ANALOGIES & ILLUSTRATIONS

representing ideas in primary science

Hilary Asoko **Max de Bóo**

Acknowledgements

The authors wish to thank:

Bob Bullock, Member of the ASE Publications Committee, and colleagues in the University of Leeds for their valued ideas and commentary on the text.

Brenda Keogh and **Stuart Naylor** for permission to use concept cartoons from *Concept Cartoons in Science Education* (2000). Sandbach, Cheshire: Millgate House Publishing.

Dr Peter Borrows, Past Chair, ASE Safeguards in Science Committee, for helpful additions and comments regarding safety.

Safety issues

For health and safety in primary school science and technology an important and useful reference is:

ASE (2001) *Be Safe!* (third edition). ISBN 0 86357 324 X

This edition supersedes the second edition of *Be Safe!* (1990) and the Scottish edition (1995). It includes new material about managing health and safety and risk assessment. It has been commended for use in England, Wales, Scotland and Northern Ireland

Published by
The Association for Science Education
College Lane
Hatfield
Herts AL10 9AA
Telephone   +44 (0)1707 283000
Fax   +44 (0)1707 266532
e-mail   ase@asehq.telme.com
website   www.ase.org.uk

Designed and typeset by Paul and Hendrina Ellis: 01780 481326
Photography by Graeme Harris: 020 8740 4929
Printed by Black Bear Press, Cambridge

ISBN   0 86357 331 2

Contents

FOREWORD

We were talking to a primary science co-ordinator. In the course of the conversation we asked, *'If you could get research done on anything in science education, what would it be?'* He said, *'How to answer questions that teachers ask, like "How do I explain evaporation to Year 5?".'*

As teachers, we spend a lot of time thinking about how to explain scientific ideas in ways that children can understand. With experience, we develop strategies which work for us, using pictures, 3-D models, drama, gestures, various kinds of analogies and so on to help children make sense of difficult concepts but we are always on the look-out for different ideas and approaches.

We decided to write this book to illustrate some principles behind introducing scientific concepts to children and some practical ideas which can be used in the classroom.

We focused on some of the ideas that researchers and teachers in projects such as CLIS (Children's Learning in Science) and SPACE (Science Processes And Concept Exploration) have shown to be difficult to teach and to learn. We have tried to offer strategies that will stimulate imagination and thoughtful discussion and result in greater understanding in science lessons through a *'minds-on'* as well as a *'hands-on'* approach.

Max de Bóo, Hilary Asoko
Autumn 2001

The authors

Max de Bóo has had extensive teaching experience as a teacher in nursery and primary schools, in teacher training and INSET. She is a national speaker and the author of several books on primary education and science.

Hilary Asoko taught in the UK and abroad before becoming a lecturer at the University of Leeds, where she is involved in the initial and in-service training of primary teachers. She is particularly interested in the teacher's role in the development of children's conceptual understanding of science.

1 Introduction

1.1 Teaching and learning science

Primary science education took a giant leap forward in the last decades of the twentieth century, with enthusiastic teachers encouraging children to be actively involved in practical investigations in the classroom. 'Doing' science has high status in lessons. However, many teachers recognise that 'doing' science, on its own, does not necessarily lead to children developing an understanding of science concepts. If children are to learn to think more scientifically, these 'tools for thinking' have to be introduced deliberately.

Developing children's understanding of the concepts of science forms the focus of this book. It is intended as a resource for teachers who want (a) to bring the ideas of science into the classroom in imaginative and useful ways and (b) to enable children to use these ideas to question, explore, interpret, explain and ponder on their experience of the world. It is not a teaching scheme but a selection of strategies, exemplified in specific contexts, which can be used to supplement, extend and enhance existing teaching.

Inevitably, a number of assumptions and beliefs, about science and about its teaching and learning, underpin the suggestions made. These are outlined below, with additional reading indicated for those who would like to explore the ideas further.

Science

Defining exactly what science is is not easy. However, one of the *products* of scientific activity is a developing body of reliable knowledge about the material world, which has a considerable impact on our daily lives. The scientific ideas and explanations which we teach in school have been developed over many years and by many people. They are the result, not only of careful observation and investigation, but also of imaginative and creative thinking. Once understood, these ideas can provide us with very useful ways of interpreting and understanding the world [1]*. However, these ideas and explanations are not self-evident. They often involve 'things' or processes – gravity, food chains, electric current, photosynthesis, particles, rays of light, evaporation – which are not directly apparent. In addition, many scientific ideas and explanations seem counter to common sense or everyday thinking, or may be difficult to imagine or hard to believe. For example, the idea that a moving object will keep moving forever in the absence of a force to stop it, may seem to go against common sense derived from experience. It can be hard to believe that the wood which makes a table has been produced from the combination of a liquid, water, and a gas, carbon dioxide. It is not surprising, therefore, that the teaching and learning of science can be challenging!

Children's developing ideas about the natural world

Children develop ideas about natural phenomena as a result of their interaction with all aspects of the physical and social world around them. Experiences whilst playing, or at school, interactions with other people, both children and adults, information from books, TV and magazines, knowledge gained through hobbies and other interests, all play a part. Studies in various countries around the world have provided information about the ideas and understandings which children of different ages develop about a wide range of topics [2]. This research suggests that the ideas which children hold are not idiosyncratic;

* Numbers in [brackets] refer to *References and further reading*, page 66.

similar patterns in the ways in which ideas develop can be found amongst children from different cultures. These patterns reflect how children make sense of their physical and social experiences. Some of the ideas which children develop have elements in common with the scientific explanations which they meet in science lessons, but other ideas which children hold may be significantly different from school science. Frequently, even after teaching, children retain their 'common sense' ideas and reject the science view.

Children learning science

A view of learning as a process in which people are actively making sense, rather than passively receiving knowledge directly and unchanged is often referred to as a 'constructivist' view of learning [3]. This helps to explain why what is taught is not necessarily what is learnt.

Many people would argue that physical experience stimulates such sense-making in children and that science should, therefore, be based in practical activity. It is true that practical activities can engage children's interest and curiosity and have a motivating effect. They allow children to explore objects, and to find out what happens in a given situation and what can affect this. However, phenomena do not explain themselves. Explanation involves mental effort and the development of ideas. Children may develop their own explanations for many of the things they encounter, with young children often categorising anything unexplainable as 'magic'. But learning science involves more than making personal sense of the physical world and so practical exploration has its limitations. Science has a powerful set of tools, in the form of networks of related concepts, for describing and explaining. Children cannot discover these for themselves from their own practical explorations, but they need access to them in order to develop their scientific thinking. Introducing children to scientific concepts, and helping them to understand and use them appropriately is thus at least as important as encouraging their own empirical enquiry. In the process, existing understanding may be challenged and may need to be reconsidered.

Teaching science

Teaching science involves opening children's eyes to new and exciting possibilities for thinking about the world. It is the teacher's responsibility to introduce useful ways of thinking about and interpreting experience, at an appropriate time, to help children to make these ideas their own and to model how to use them. However, as has already been discussed, children come to science lessons with ideas which they have constructed from personal experience and from ideas picked up from others. Science ideas may seem quite contradictory to their understandings or involve concepts which are unfamiliar and abstract. This means that introducing a scientific way of thinking, in a form that children can understand and appreciate, can be difficult. Explaining the science view is much more than simply 'telling' children what they should believe.

It involves making connections between the science ideas being presented and children's personal experience and thinking. 'What' is told is clearly important, but when and how ideas are introduced and explored can be crucial, as is knowing when to stop!

When introducing new ideas, a teacher needs an awareness of a range of experiences and activities which can provide opportunities for children and teacher to explore, investigate and discuss the relevant science, as well as strategies for maximising the potential for learning from these activities.

In planning how to introduce the science, the teacher therefore needs to think about:

❑ how to 'prepare the ground' and create a need for new ideas and explanations.

Can questions be raised about things taken for granted in everyday experience? Can experimental results be generated which require interpreting, or existing ideas be challenged and found to be inadequate?

❏ what can be assumed and what must be introduced.

What experiences are children likely to be familiar with which are relevant to the ideas to be introduced? How are they likely to be thinking about these? Is this thinking helpful in terms of the science ideas to be introduced? Are some of their ideas likely to be contrary to the science view which needs to be developed? What are children unlikely to know?

❏ what is essential to the 'scientific story'.

What must be focused on or emphasised? What may be distracting or can be left out?

❏ how the story can be presented.

What can be used to represent 'invisible' things? What words, actions, analogies, diagrams, drawings, props, etc. might be helpful? How can links be made to existing thinking?

❏ what problems in understanding might arise.

What is difficult? What makes it difficult? How can problems be dealt with or avoided?

Providing new ideas and alternative views is only the first stage in developing understanding. The teacher then needs to provide opportunities for ideas to be explored, used and revisited in a range of contexts, through practical work and discussion-based activity [4]. He/she also needs to model for children how to use the ideas in scientific reasoning and argument.

Making scientific sense in the classroom involves making links between ideas and explanations, experiences of phenomena and events, and more systematic investigation (Figure **1.1**). Teaching could start with any one of these and the balance between them will depend on the demands of the topic, the background of the learners and the intentions of the teacher. Ultimately, learning science involves constructing the ideas, explanations and models of science for yourself and recognising where and when it is appropriate to use them. Teachers need to use all means at their disposal to make the ideas of science understandable and relate them to the children's existing knowledge and experience. We hope that this book provides some useful suggestions for doing this.

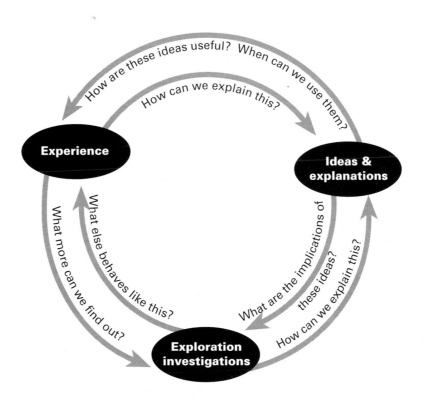

1.1   *The experience, exploration and explanation wheel*

1.2 Representing ideas: a word about illustrations, models and analogies

Ideas are abstract 'things'. No-one can see an idea. In order to communicate an idea, it has to be represented in some way, for example by words, symbols, gestures, actions, pictures, diagrams, physical models, formulae, singly or in combination. If the idea is to be communicated effectively, the representation needs to be well-chosen, clear and concise.

Analogies, models and metaphors are all representations used to convey meaning. However, these terms are difficult to define and the distinctions between them are difficult to make with any precision. The word 'model', for example, might refer to a physical model, such as a globe or a model of an eye. It could refer to a conceptual model – the network of ideas an individual holds in relation to a particular phenomenon. Many children, for example, have a conceptual model of electricity as a substance which flows into a house through a socket, a model which they have developed by analogy with gas and water supplies; or they may think of the sky as a defined surface above the earth, like a ceiling. Scientific models and the theories associated with them are networks of ideas, developed over time, and used to explain and make predictions about natural phenomena, for example the wave model of light, or the particulate theory of matter (for detailed discussion see ASE, undated [5]). Using models depends on analogical reasoning, which requires the recognition of similarities between two situations. It is a way of making sense of something new in terms of existing ideas and experience. Reasoning by analogy is fundamental to cognition and children are capable of it from a very early age (Goswami [6]).

Representations, both verbal and non-verbal, are central to developing thinking both in science itself and in the teaching and learning of science. The relationship between language and thinking for both scientists and learners is explored in Sutton [7]. In science teaching the kinds of things which may need to be represented include:

- ❏ abstract concepts, such as electric current, force, food web
- ❏ processes, such as growth, evaporation, photosynthesis
- ❏ scale, in relation to very large or very small things such as the distance from the Sun to the Earth, the size of a bacterium or the number of molecules in a glass of water (de Bóo and Asoko [8]).

Although words alone could be used, physical representations have a number of advantages in a teaching situation. For example they can:

- ❏ capture and focus attention
- ❏ provide a stimulus for discussion
- ❏ allow different parts to be considered separately and then related to the whole
- ❏ provide a stimulus which requires effort to interpret and so aid thinking
- ❏ require the identification of similarities and differences which aids understanding
- ❏ stimulate creative thinking
- ❏ provide something memorable and understandable which can be drawn upon later to support thinking.

This can be illustrated by considering the use of the 'Smartie' analogy for electricity (*see* **A2** page 50). Use of an analogy such as this draws on children's existing knowledge and experience as a basis for developing understanding of a new idea, often called the 'target'. The direct involvement of the children can be motivating and make the experience memorable. Links can be explicitly made between the physical elements of the representation, the components of the circuit and the explanatory ideas to be developed. Exploring the similarities and differences between the representation and the circuit aids understanding. For example, the container as the source of Smarties is similar to the battery as source of energy, but the current requires a 'push' from the battery, whereas children can move on their own. Using the analogy may stimulate children to make links to other ideas they have, for example by thinking of current as being like a conveyor belt. In later work with circuits, children may draw on ideas from the representation to aid thinking, for example when considering what would happen if the resistance of a circuit is increased.

Some difficulties in using representations include:

❏ children may need support in linking the representation to the 'target' situation, e.g. moving children may not be linked to current

❏ children may remember the event but not what it represents, e.g. they remember eating the Smarties, but not any connection to electricity!

❏ irrelevant or misleading features may be incorporated into the new way of thinking, e.g. children do not stop simultaneously as current in all parts of the circuit does

❏ the representation is not the 'target' situation – nothing behaves like electricity except electricity.

In selecting representations to use, teachers therefore need to consider:

❏ what is represented and how well?

❏ what is not represented?

❏ what might be confusing?

❏ what are the limitations of the representation?

❏ will children be able to understand it easily, does it need prior knowledge?

Finally, it should be remembered that it is not the representation alone which produces understanding but the intellectual effort of relating it to the 'target' situation and the talk which supports this. There are no guarantees that, however well chosen and used, representations will lead to the desired understanding. Even when a representation does give insight into a scientific way of thinking, unless the use of a new way of understanding is modelled by the teacher and practised by the children it will soon be forgotten.

1.3 Using this book

Chapters 2 to 7 deal with aspects of the school curriculum for science which can be challenging for learners.

Each chapter follows a similar format, which is described below.

Curriculum references

References are given to relevant sections of the Programme of Study of the National Curriculum for England and Wales (DfEE, 1999) and to the Scottish National Guidelines (1999), as well as to the QCA Scheme of Work for Science for Key Stages 1 and 2 (1998). These are for broad guidance only and material from any section can be used whenever appropriate.

What's the problem?

In this section we outline what can be challenging for learners in relation to the particular topic. In general terms this is often related to moving from *knowing what happens* in a particular situation to developing a more scientific understanding of *how this can be explained.* Developing such explanations often involves being able to use abstract ideas, with which children are unfamiliar.

What might children think?

Children bring to their learning of science experiences and ideas which influence how they understand the science presented to them in school. Some of these are useful and can be utilised and built on by the teacher. However, some experiences and commonsense explanations may be in conflict with the science and are likely to hinder learning. In this section we identify some of the main ideas and experiences which a teacher may find it helpful to be aware of.

The challenge for the teacher

In general terms, the challenge for the teacher lies in recognising which of the children's existing ideas and experiences can be used and developed in teaching and which may be counter-productive. Some ideas can be tested practically, but some cannot, and must be tested through reasoning. The teacher also needs to know how to make specific teaching interventions to introduce new ideas and to be able to relate these ideas to everyday experience and to practical activities in the classroom.

Vocabulary issues

Learning science involves learning to use the language of science in appropriate ways. Sometimes this means learning new words and ways of talking. At other times it involves a recognition that words in everyday use, such as force or weight, have specific meanings in a science context. Scientific ways of thinking and talking need to be modelled by the teacher and practised by the children.

Possible starting points

In this section some guidance is given about suitable experiences which might be used to focus children's attention on relevant aspects of the situation under consideration.

Sometimes several possibilities are given. It is not intended that all should be used, rather that the teacher will select ideas which seem most useful and relevant to the particular children concerned. Often these activities provide opportunities for checking whether necessary prerequisite experiences and ideas are available to the children.

Focus

This is the most important section of each topic. It provides suggestions for introducing new ideas or lines of reasoning which help children towards a more scientific view. Again these are suggestions from which teachers can select approaches most suited to the children concerned. It is very important to recognise the role of teacher input here. It is not the activity itself which stimulates new learning, but the way it is used by the teacher. The activity provides a context in which ideas can be introduced and explored, with the teacher providing ideas, making links, asking questions and stimulating thinking.

Points to make clear

Identifies potential causes of confusion, together with points for teachers to be aware of in using the strategies.

Use of ideas, applications and extensions

Children make sense of new ideas by having to use them. Here we provide some suggestions for how this might be done. Activities in this section provide opportunities for children to use new ideas to explain observations or to make predictions. Some allow investigation of the implications of ideas through investigations or 'thought experiments'. Others stimulate the discussion or application of ideas.

Relating ideas back to everyday experiences and making links between related contexts will help to develop understanding and consolidate learning.

References and further reading

References (numbered [1], [2], etc.) are provided at the end of the book. These provide sources of information about children's thinking or about the use of particular activities in practice. Additional reading material is provided for some chapters.

2 Green plants

2.1 Growth

National Curriculum reference
Sc2 Life processes and living things
Pupils should be taught
KS1	**3a**	to recognise that plants need light and water to grow
	3b	to recognise and name the leaf, flower, stem and root of flowering plants
KS2	**1b**	that the life processes common to plants include growth
	3a	the effect of light, air, water and temperature on plant growth

Scottish National Guidelines
Environmental studies. The processes of life
Level B recognise stages in the life cycles of familiar plants and animals
identify the main parts of flowering plants
Level C describe the broad functions of the main parts of flowering plants
Level D describe the main stages in flowering plant reproduction

Relevant QCA unit
1B	Growing plants
3B	Helping plants grow well

What's the problem?
- How do we recognise a 'plant'?
- Is a plant alive?
- Where does the 'stuff' come from for the plant to grow?
- Where do plants grow best? Why?

What might children think?

Nature of growth Children are likely to:
- doubt that a tree is a plant (too big or too '*hard*')
- be unwilling to classify things we eat as plants but refer to them as something else, e.g. '*It's a vegetable not a plant!*'
- think that growth just '*happens*'
- think that the stem and leaves come from inside the seed or under the ground. Younger children may think that the roots/shoots simply push the plant upwards.
- talk about the plant incorporating soil, compost, minerals, water and air
- think of growth as simply getting '*bigger*' rather than a range of developing features.

Conditions for growth Children are likely to:
- know that plants need water as a *condition* for growth, i.e. not incorporated into the plant. Younger children may say that soil is needed as well as the Sun, although the Sun may not be thought of as 'light' energy or radiation.
- think that the most important condition for growth is soil, then warmth/heat and air and light. Older children do not always make connections with seeds that germinate in the dark.

2.1 *Ideas about how plants become bigger or heavier*

reduced, from Keogh and Naylor, *Concept Cartoons in Science Education*, 2000

Growing time

❑ Children are divided into those who think that growth occurs little by little all the time and those who think growth happens in the morning/day or at night. Growth is seen as an endless process or something that stops at a predetermined stage.

The challenge for the teacher

Teachers need to convince children that:

❑ plants can grow without soil

❑ plants can only grow for a limited time without light and water

❑ plants either stop growing or grow very slowly in cold conditions

❑ many plants do not grow in extreme conditions, i.e. with excess water, etc.

❑ growth can be measured by increase in mass as well as size.

Vocabulary issues

Growing equated with simply getting 'bigger'; or with getting food from the soil and 'sucking up' or 'drinking' water.

Possible starting points

(This focuses on plant growth rather than seed germination. The concept of stored 'food' in a seed, bulb or tuber is not dealt with here.)

1 Discuss the ideas in the concept cartoon on plant growth (Figure **2.1**).

2 Bring in a few plants for observation, e.g. sprouted runner beans, a begonia, a geranium/pelargonium, an amaryllis (winter months), and discuss (a) what conditions the plants need to help them to grow and (b) what is happening inside the plant to make it grow. Investigate growing conditions.

Focus | ## Plants grow without soil.
Plants need water, (air), and light to grow.

1 Show growth. Grow some plants without soil (e.g. cress on blotting paper or felt cloth, mung beans in a sprouting pot (Figure **2.2**), broad bean shoots between blotting paper and sides of jam jars, pelargoniums in hydroponic gel). Weighing the plant + container at the start and at intervals during the growth topic period as well as measuring height will demonstrate growth without soil. The number of leaves and size of leaf area in the leafy plants could be measured too.

2 Observe, record and explain the growth of the plants growing under different conditions.

Focus | ## Growth and parts of a plant

1 Represent a growing plant in card or felt, with removable parts: seed (bulb or tuber), roots, shoot, stem + leaves, stem + more leaves, flower and flower parts. Assemble on a mounting board or cloth (pieces could be Velcro'd); name labels could be added. The level of difficulty and number of parts will depend on the age and experience of the children. This could become a game with numbered pieces and dice or be used as an aid to the story of growth (Figure **2.3**).

2 Represent the growth of a plant as in (**1**), using a series of overhead transparencies (OHTs) overlaid to show growth. Coloured OHTs are best for this and are readily photocopiable (if not in school) in any good reprographics shop.

3 Make a 3-dimensional model of a growing plant, starting from a string-rooted seed in a plastic pot, cardboard tubing for the stem, card or paper leaves, etc. This could be a set task for Designing and Making, with additional objectives such as: the plant has to be freestanding and stable, has to attract insects and have a method of seed dispersal.

4 Dramatise plant growth in movement (such as 'What's the time, Mr Wolf?'). Some children act as seeds or small plants, others as the Sun, the rain (the air?). The appearance or absence of any one of these (show or conceal the symbol) triggers growth, slows it down or stops growth altogether. If children question the need for air, ask if plants can grow out in space.

5 Read traditional and other stories: *The Great Big Enormous Turnip*, *Jack and the Beanstalk*. Discuss probabilities of such growth.

6 Represent growth with construction kits that make a plant 'grow' day by day.

7 Show time-lapse photography of growth from TV, video or the internet.

Conventional representation

Labelled drawings are generally used to show snapshots of growth (Figure **2.4**).

Points to make clear

❏ The soil itself does not make plants grow. Soil acts as an anchor for the plant and also as a medium for stored water and certain essential minerals (nutrients) to be taken in by the fine roots.

❏ There are many changes that occur inside the plant that we can't see, e.g. water and carbon dioxide are combined in the presence of sunlight to make materials for new growth.

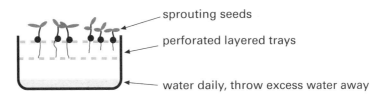

sprouting seeds

perforated layered trays

water daily, throw excess water away

2.2 *Sprouting seeds*

2.3 *A plant-parts model*

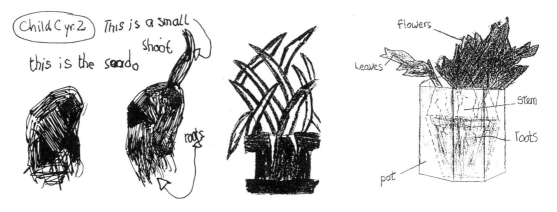

2.4 *Children's drawings of plants with labels, child aged seven on the left, child aged nine on the right*

2.2 Photosynthesis

National Curriculum reference
Sc2 Life processes and living things
Pupils should be taught:
KS2   **3b** the role of the leaf in producing new material for growth
Level 6   (respiration and) photosynthesis

Scottish National Guidelines
Environmental studies. Interaction of living things with their environment
Level D explain how response to changes in the environment might increase the chances of survival
          give examples of how plants and animals are suited to the environment
Level E identify the raw materials, conditions and products of photosynthesis

Relevant QCA unit
6A   Interdependence and adaptation

What's the problem?

■ Where does the 'stuff' come from which makes up the plant?

■ What is a leaf for? What does a leaf do?

What might children think?

Children may think that:

❏ 'food' is an edible thing, visible and tangible

❏ 'food' for plants comes from the soil or the roots – they suck it up

❏ air is not used by plants – or that plants and animals use air in opposite ways

❏ 'plants grow food for us, people – not for their own growth'

❏ plants 'drink' water and 'breathe' carbon dioxide, but these are not changed in the process

❏ photosynthesis is a substance, rather than a process.

The challenge for the teacher

The teacher needs to convince children that:

❏ the 'stuff' (the growth material) is produced in the leaves

❏ plants can grow without soil

❏ plants use light energy to combine a gas in the air (colourless, odourless, 'invisible' carbon dioxide) and liquid water into a solid 'food', a kind of sugar

❏ plants use the sugar-food they have made to help themselves to grow and reproduce

❏ people eat plants for food (and animals that have eaten plant food) because we cannot *make* food for ourselves – only green plants can do that

❏ photosynthesis is a process like a chemical reaction.

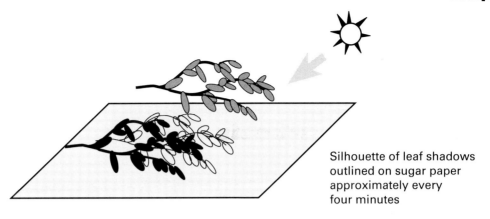

2.5 *A tracing onto sugar paper of the leaf shadows cast by strong sunlight*

2.6 *Variation in leaf shape and size*

Vocabulary issues

Food may be thought of as solid or liquid nutrients only, an idea encouraged by the 'plant food' and fertilisers sold in garden centres. Plants and trees make 'food' for us/people (i.e. that is their *purpose*). In a biological sense, 'food' means something that can provide energy or material for growth.

Focus

Plants need light and grow towards the light

1 Demonstrate leaf cover. On a bright day with shadows, stand under a tree in full leaf and assess how much light gets through the canopy. Put pieces of sugar paper on the ground, draw round the shadows created by the light that comes through the canopy and discuss the reasons why the tree has so many leaves (e.g. greatest area exposed to sunlight radiation, weight of individual leaves, etc.) (Figure **2.5**).

2 Explore as many leaves as possible from different trees (e.g. horse chestnut, beech, sycamore, larch, etc.) and classify them by colour, shape, size, or other criteria suggested by the children. Discuss the adaptations each tree uses for its leaves to 'catch' as much light as possible (i.e. variation in plants, response to local environment, micro-climate, etc.) (Figure **2.6**).

3 Demonstrate movement. Set up some green leafy pot plants on a windowsill such that sunlight traverses from East to West during the day. Observe the movement of the leaves towards the light. Alternatively, set up a small black screen beside the plants so that light falls mostly from one direction and observe the leaves change position to face the light (i.e. living things respond to their environment, upper surface of leaves compared with under-surface for photosynthesis, etc.) (Figure **2.7**).

4 Demonstrate the effect of limited access to light. Cover parts of the leaves on a pot plant with black strips of paper, using paper-clips or masking tape. Place on a sunny shelf for a week. Remove the black paper strips and observe the differences in the leaves. Chlorophyll (the green pigment) traps light energy and begins the process of photosynthesis. Without light energy the potential for photosynthesis is inhibited.

Focus ## Photosynthesis is a chemical reaction between a gas and a liquid, requiring energy (sunlight)

HAZARD

1 Demonstrate a chemical reaction: add vinegar to baking powder (sodium bicarbonate), or discuss the changes when we fry a raw egg.
All of these involve a transfer of energy and represent an irreversible change.

2 Illustrate change. Observe and describe a separated egg, especially the egg-white (liquid). Predict what will happen if energy is used (+ an egg whisk) to mix air (gases) into the liquid egg-white. Describe the whipped egg-white now (semi-solid?) and the difference between baking unbeaten and beaten egg-white.
CARE: good hygiene needed (salmonella risk).

3 Dramatise a 'Leaf Factory' with a small designated green leaf area (Figure **2.8**). Some children act as Carbon Dioxide particles in the air near the leaf, some children as Water particles near the stem of the leaf. Two children have symbols for Rain and the Sun. When it rains (Rain symbol shown), some Water particles move into the leaf area. When the Sun shines (light energy), some of the Carbon Dioxide particles join up with Water particles and become plant food, and the leaf area enlarges. Discuss what happens to the particles when the leaf dies.

Points to make clear

❏ Whisking air into egg-white is creating a mixture, not a chemical reaction, but it shows that air and liquid can mix together and make something different.

❏ The analogy of the leaf factory only shows a small part of the process and doesn't indicate either the number of particles required to make plant food (sugar) or the role of chlorophyll. It is simplifying the process to focus on the combination of CO_2 gas and water.

❏ Growth and photosynthesis do not happen just when it rains.

❏ Growth does not only occur in the leaf, it also occurs elsewhere in the plant.

Conventional representation of photosynthesis

This is usually shown on a plant with roots; in sunlight; with arrows and labels surrounding a leaf (Figure **2.9**).

Use of ideas, applications and extensions

❏ What would happen if the plants were given lots more light and/or water and/or heat? Does 'more' always equal 'better'? Would the plants grow like Jack's beanstalk? If not, why not?

❏ Can the children think of places where plants cannot survive and why? (e.g. caves – no light; the desert – no water; the Moon – no carbon dioxide or water.)

❏ What would happen to plants if they had no 'anchor' roots buried deep in the soil? Explore the analogy and meaning of 'anchor' roots.

2.7   *Orientation of leaves in growing plant towards sunlight to maximise photosynthesis*

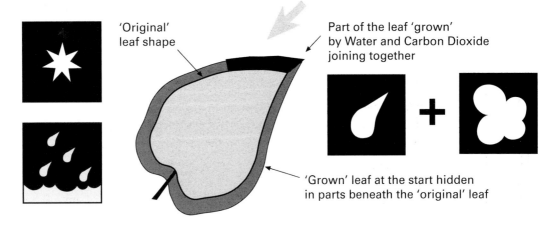

'Original' leaf shape

Part of the leaf 'grown' by Water and Carbon Dioxide joining together

'Grown' leaf at the start hidden in parts beneath the 'original' leaf

2.8   *The 'Leaf Factory' game*

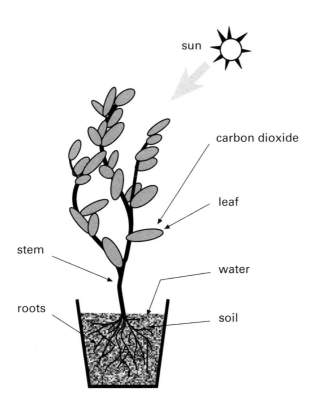

sun

carbon dioxide

leaf

stem

water

roots

soil

2.9   *Conventional representation of photosynthesis*

2.3 Food chains and food webs

National Curriculum reference
Sc2 Life processes and living things
Pupils should be taught:
KS1   3a to recognise that plants need light and water to grow
KS2   1c to make links between life processes in familiar animals and plants and the environments in which they are found
        5b about the different plants and animals found in diverse habitats
        5d to use food chains to show feeding relationships in a habitat
        5e about how nearly all food chains start with a green plant

Scottish National Guidelines
Environmental studies. Interaction of living things with their environment
Level B   construct simple food chains
Level C   explain how living things and the environment can be protected and give examples
Level E   construct and interpret simple food webs and make prediction of the consequences of change
          give examples of physical factors that affect the distribution of living things

Relevant QCA unit
4A   Habitats
5B   Life cycles
6A   Interdependence and adaptation

What's the problem?

■ Do we really *need* plants?

What might children think?

Children are likely to:

❑ find it difficult to believe that all animals, including humans, ultimately depend on green plants for survival

❑ think of food chains as linear, rather than cyclical and that animals on apparently higher levels in the chain prey on all the animals and plants below them.

The challenge for the teacher

Teachers need to convince children that:

❑ all animals depend on green plants

❑ there are *very many* green plants; there are *some* herbivores that eat plants and a *few* carnivores that eat herbivores and plants

❑ some animals, including humans, eat plants and animals for food

❑ plants do not grow for our personal survival – plants grow for their own survival.

2.10 *Animal and plant concept cartoon*

reduced, from Keogh and Naylor, *Concept Cartoons in Science Education*, 2000

Vocabulary issues

Food is edible only; chains thought of as linear only, web is equated with spiders, carnivorous equals savage, beastly, and there is confusion with the scientific meaning of dependency, herbivore, omnivore, prey and predator; and the significance of directional arrows in a food web. Some children will be unclear about the terms 'producer', 'prey' and 'predator'.

Possible starting points

1 Show a bunch of grass and discuss the possibility of living by eating the food made by, and stored in, the grass.

2 Discuss the concept cartoon of animals and plants (Figure **2.10**).

3 Make concept maps and discuss words that could link the chosen objects. For instance: (a) individual concept maps of the things children eat and where the different foods come from originally; (b) group concept maps for some of the following: chickens, hawks, dogs, dolphins, whales, squirrels, pigs, ants, snakes. *This information may need to be researched.*

Focus	**Population growth and survival depend on the availability of food on which that population feeds**

1 Dramatise population growth and dependencies by playing the Eco-game [1] (see Figure **2.11**). Let 20 to 24 children *represent* two lettuces each (green cards in each hand). Five children can be rabbits (brown card) and there is one fox (red card). Each rabbit has to eat two lettuces per day (collect two green cards), the fox has to eat one rabbit every three days. Every day six new lettuces grow back (three children). No rabbit can go without food (collect green cards) for more than three days (dies), the fox cannot go for more than five days without food (dies). Use a tambourine to indicate the end and beginning of each day.

Discuss what happens. What is the situation after five days? After ten days?

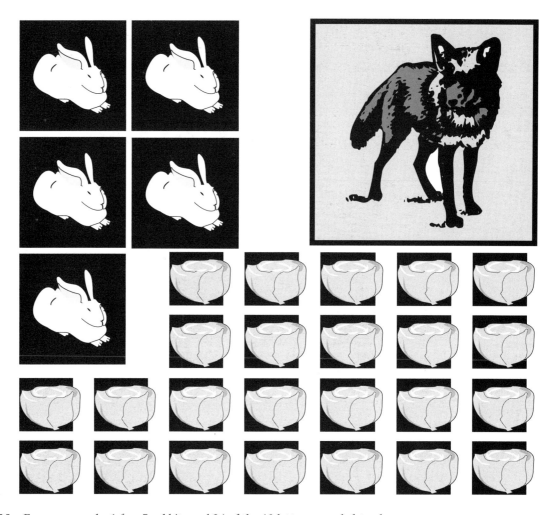

2.11 *Eco-game cards: 1 fox, 5 rabbits and 24 of the 48 lettuces needed to play*

2 Try the game again: What happens if a drought or a flood kills off 20 lettuces on the second day? What if the farmer kills three rabbits? If fox-hunters kill the fox? How often would the rabbits need to breed to maintain their population? How often would the fox?

Points to make clear

❏ Children may say food comes from the supermarket or the country of origin – accept and approve these answers as they are not 'wrong'. Ask the children to elaborate.

❏ Some children may not know that potatoes (in potato crisps) grow from green plants or that wheat (in bread) is also a green plant.

❏ Children may not know that some marine animals feed on green algae – a type of green plant that grows in the sea (seaweed).

❏ In the Eco-game, remind children that the feeding system is not as simple as the game suggests: rabbits feed on several green plants and foxes eat various small animals. Rabbits may reproduce several times during Spring and Summer; foxes generally once or twice a year only.

Use of ideas, applications and extensions

❏ What happens when the animals in the game die – what happens to the 'food' their bodies are made of?

❏ Play an alternative Eco-game (as described in Bailey [1]).

3 The human body

3.1 The heart and circulation

National Curriculum reference
Sc2 Life processes and living things
Pupils should be taught:
KS2   **2c** that the heart acts as a pump to circulate the blood through vessels around the body, including through the lungs
2d about the effect of exercise and rest on pulse rate

Scottish National Guidelines
Environmental studies. The processes of life
Level C   describe the broad functions of the organs of the human body

Relevant QCA unit
5A   Keeping healthy

What's the problem?

Through practical investigation children can learn how to take a pulse, and can measure and compare resting and exercising pulse rates. That pulse rate increases with exercise is not difficult to demonstrate. However, questions which cannot be answered through practical activity include:

❏ what is your pulse?

❏ why does your heart beat?

❏ why does it sometimes beat faster than at others?

Answering these questions involves drawing on an understanding of the differing demands for energy and how the body responds to these. Links need to be made between physical activity and the heart and its function. The teacher therefore needs to bear in mind that a long-term goal is to develop an understanding of an inter-related group of organs, the circulatory system, which can be used to explain physiological effects. Such knowledge underpins an understanding of health issues related to exercise, diet and smoking.

What might children think?

Children are likely to have some knowledge of the organs of the body. They will almost certainly know that they have a heart, brain, blood, bones and muscles. However, knowledge of where these and other organs are in the body, what they do and how they inter-relate is likely to be sketchy. For example, children may think of blood as just filling up spaces in the body rather than being contained in vessels.

Personal experience and hospital dramas on television mean that children are likely to bring to their learning relevant, but limited, knowledge and awareness. For example they are likely to:

❏ be aware of what happens to their bodies during exercise (heart beating faster, sweating, breathlessness) but not know why this should be

❏ know that blood comes from a cut, but not how it gets there

❏ know that a person can bleed to death and, perhaps, that blood can be transfused but not why blood is so important

❏ know that if your heart stops beating you may die, but see heart-beat as a sign of life, rather than knowing what the heart does and how this supports life

❏ know that muscles are used in exercise, but not that muscles need a supply of food and oxygen to function.

The challenge for the teacher

The teacher needs to:

❏ develop knowledge of the components of the circulatory system. These are not directly accessible to children and so must be represented in some way

❏ develop awareness that these components work together in a co-ordinated way to respond to the needs of the body, such as when exercising

❏ make simple links between physical activity and the body's need for food and oxygen, with the blood as the transport medium.

Possible starting points

Depending on children's existing knowledge and experience, and teacher preference, it may be appropriate to focus initially on one of the following:

❏ the individual components (heart, blood, lungs) and what they do, leading on to how these operate as a system (useful links might be made to hi-fi or computer systems in which a number of different components are linked together to perform a task) and then relating this to what happens in exercise

❏ the observable effects of exercise and then consider what is needed during exercise and how the body is able to meet these needs

❏ what the body takes in (food and oxygen) and the need for a transport system to get these to where they are needed.

Focus ## The circulatory system

1 Explore and discuss pumps with which children are familiar, such as bicycle pumps, balloon pumps and water pumps, all of which are needed to move fluids from one place to another. Stress that, if we need to move blood round the body, we need a pump and this is what the heart does. (Water pumps are usually accessible in KS1 classrooms or in the Nursery.)
The pumping action of the heart can be heard (with a stethoscope) and felt (at pulse points).

2 Diagrams, such as Figure **3.1**, are useful because they give a simplified picture of the components and their relationship to each other. If presented by the teacher as being like a map used for the London Underground, or bus routes, children can recognise that they show paths which blood can take (all of which are one-way).

3 Use animated representations, for example, from video, CD-Roms and the internet.

4 Use anatomical or other models. The functioning of the circulatory system, at its basic level of a pump and a system of tubes, can be represented by a simple physical model made from a soap dispenser (Figure **3.2**).
Note this can also be used as a circuit model – the similarities are the one-way flow, a defined pathway and the need for something to provide a push.

5 Drama can be used to illustrate or reinforce the idea of a system which transports materials to parts of the body such as the muscles. For example, children can circulate as blood along a defined route, passing through areas labelled lungs, heart and muscles. In the lungs they pick up oxygen, represented by pieces of red card or multilink blocks and deposit it in the muscles where it is used. Greater demand for

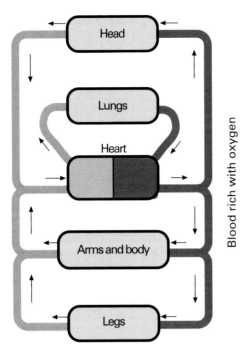

3.1   *Heart and circulation model*

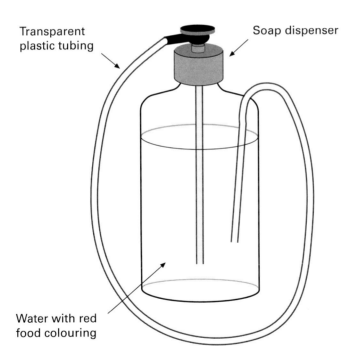

3.2   *Soap dispenser model of circulation*

adapted from Newton, L, and Newton, D. [1996] Young children and understanding electricity. *Primary Science Review,* **41**, 14–16.

oxygen by exercising muscles means that more must be taken in by the lungs (hence faster breathing) and faster transport (hence faster heartbeat). Variations on this can include the transport of food and carbon dioxide, or the inclusion of other organs.

Points to make clear

❏ The conventional representation of oxygenated blood in red and deoxygenated in blue does not mean that this is the actual colour of the blood.

❏ Representing oxygenated blood on the right side of a diagram and deoxygenated blood on the left does not mean that the left side of the body has only oxygenated blood.

❏ Only a few main blood vessels are represented on diagrams (like a map which only shows motorways) but these have branches, which have further branches which go to (and come from) all parts of the body.

Use of ideas, applications and extensions

Children can be asked to try to use their knowledge of the circulatory system to explain real-life situations such as first aid, and exercise, for example:

1 Acting out the scene of an accident and providing a commentary on why doctors/ paramedics check for a pulse and bleeding, and what happens inside a person whose heart stops.

2 Carrying out various activities (e.g. walking, skipping, sitting down) and describing what changes they think are happening inside their bodies.

4 Materials

4.1 Solids, liquids and gases

National Curriculum reference
Sc3 Materials and their properties
Pupils should be taught:
KS2 **1e** to recognise differences between solids, liquids and gases, in terms of ease of flow and maintenance of shape and volume
  3e to use knowledge of solids, liquids and gases to decide how mixtures might be separated
Level 6 that matter is made up of particles and to describe the differences between the arrangement and movement of particles in solids, liquids and gases

Scottish National Guidelines
Environmental studies. Materials from Earth
Level B Explain why water conservation is so important
Level C Describe the differences between solids, liquids and gases
  Give everyday uses of solids, liquids and gases

Relevant QCA unit
1C Sorting and using materials
2D Grouping and changing materials
3C Characteristics of materials
4D Solids, liquids and how they can be separated
5C Gases around us

What's the problem?

■ Learning to think of all materials as 'matter' – including air and water as well as wood and metal.

■ Accepting that some materials appear to contradict their allocated category, e.g. solid sand flows rather like a liquid.

■ Accepting that matter can be there (e.g. gas) even if we cannot see it.

■ Recognising that classification systems have 'fuzzy boundaries'.

What might children think?

About materials Children are likely to:
❏ equate 'materials' with 'fabrics' only

❏ think that all solids are 'strong' or 'hard' and reject cotton wool and sponges as 'solids' (can be squashed) and pourable solids such as sand and flour

❏ think that water is the only liquid; associate liquids with drinking; think that all liquids are 'runny'. Viscous liquids like treacle, and colourless, dangerous liquids like white spirit, may be confusing.

❏ focus on the *object* rather than what it is made from.

About gases Children are likely to:

❏ think that gases have no weight and that they will always rise or float to the surface; think of a cup as 'empty'; think that air is good but 'gases' are toxic (as in a gas cooker).

❏ be confused by the idea of invisible gases. Gases and 'air' are seen as being in specific locations – 'around people' or in a room or the playground where the people are. Children may not think of gases or air as filling the space; they think it is the action of the nose that makes the gas perceptible.

❏ assume that wind and moving air are different ('We don't breathe wind').

The challenge for the teacher

The teacher needs to convince children that:

❏ solids can be soft, stiff, flexible, granular or powdery

❏ not all liquids are water

❏ some liquids are viscous or coloured

❏ not all liquids are safe to drink

❏ air is real, has substance and has mass, as do other invisible gases

❏ some gases are safe and some are toxic

❏ gases can spread everywhere

❏ wind is moving air.

Vocabulary issues

The word 'materials' is equated with fabrics or building materials; 'solid' with hard, strong; 'runny' with non-viscous; 'gas' with toxic; invisible things 'don't have weight/ mass'. Kitchen foil sometimes erroneously equated with *tin* foil – it is largely *aluminium* foil.

Possible starting points

1 Sort materials into solids and liquids (and possibly gases).

2 Explore and discuss the differences between groups.

3 Discuss how we know something is a solid, liquid or gas.

4 Investigate differences between groups.

Choosing examples carefully will help to reduce children's confusion of the object with the material it is made from. Whenever possible, we suggest using pieces of material, such as a piece of plastic yogurt pot. Where not possible, remind children of the focus. Examples might include:

❏ **solids** – wood, metal (stiff or flexible), stone, plastic, Plasticine, sponge, ice, sand, flour, cotton wool

❏ **liquids** – water, vegetable oil, black treacle, vinegar, liquid paint, fizzy drink, ink, tomato ketchup, washing-up liquid

❏ **gases** – balloon full of air, helium balloon, aerosol *(CARE)*, Olbas oil or perfume.

CARE – show the children how to smell carefully by wafting the smell from the open bottles towards their noses.

Particles with energy to move can be shown by stirring a bowlful of dried peas with a spoon, giving them energy slowly or vigorously.

Focus ## Matter can be found in three different states

1 Illustrate compressibility, shape and volume. Fill syringes with air, water and sand. Predict and discuss what happens when the syringes are 'emptied' in water and in air, or sealed with a finger and compressed (Figure **4.1**). What does this tell us about the spaces between particles?

4.1 *Syringes: different states of matter*

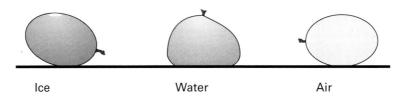

4.2 *Balloons with air and water*

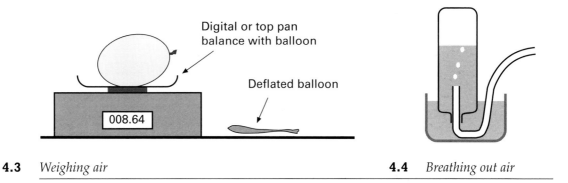

4.3 *Weighing air*   **4.4** *Breathing out air*

2 Illustrate the characteristics (shape/volume) of different states. Fill two balloons with water, one frozen (two or three days in a freezer). Fill a third balloon with air and discuss the characteristics of all three balloons. Predict and discuss the balloons being 'popped' (Figure **4.2**).

Note: using a liquid other than water in balloon (2) would help to avoid the misconception that 'air' is 'water' as a gas (use a syringe and vinegar or vegetable oil to fill the balloon).

Focus **Air exists, air is 'something'. Gases occupy space**

1 Explore and discuss bubble wrap 'bubbles' and bouncy castles.

2 'Show' air: blow up a balloon and let the air out – 'something' goes in and comes out.

3 'Weigh' air: use two large balloons – one deflated, the other full of air. Predict and discuss what happens when the balloons are weighed. This is best done on a top-pan balance with digital display: the masses are very small but it will show there is more air in the inflated balloon (Figure **4.3**).

4 Breathe air: invert a large transparent container full of water over a stand in a big dish or bowl half-full of water. Connect a tube with one end in the container and the other outside to blow into. Use it to show that we breathe out gas. The container can be calibrated roughly (Figure **4.4**).

CARE – take care with hygiene, and asthmatic children. Shared mouthpieces need to be disinfected with Milton for 30 minutes.

HAZARD

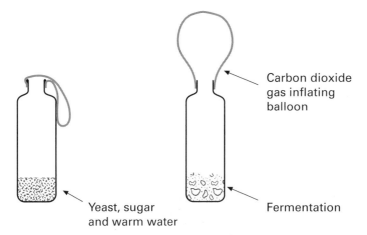

4.5 *Collecting carbon dioxide*

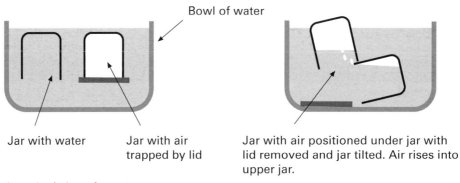

4.6 *'Pouring' air under water*

5 Show gas: make a mixture of dried yeast, sugar and warm water in a milk bottle with a large balloon over the top of the bottle to show carbon dioxide gas collecting in the balloon (Figure **4.5**).

6 'Catch' some air in a plastic bag and seal. Examine the bag by feel, then let the air out.

7 'Pour' air from one container to another container under water (Figure **4.6**).

8 Squash paper tissue into the bottom of a transparent pot or jar. Invert the pot and push down onto water in a clear glass bowl (or similar). Why does the paper stay dry? (Figure **4.7**).

Focus **All matter is made of particles whose behaviour and energy levels are different in the different states**

1 Represent solids, liquids and gases in three transparent boxes or containers: one filled completely with small wooden beads, the second half full such that the beads can roll around, the third with a few wooden beads fastened on threads and suspended from the lid in different places and different heights (Figure **4.8**).

2 Use a large transparent container with a lid; two to three cupfuls of small polystyrene balls, a wooden spoon or cardboard 'paddle' and a battery-operated cooling fan. When still, the balls represent the solid. Stirring with the paddle (giving additional energy) represents the liquid state. Agitating with the fan (further energy) represents the gaseous state (Figure **4.9**).

Note: when agitating, care is needed to close up the lid as much as possible and protect mouths and noses.

HAZARD

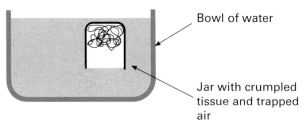

4.7 *Air takes up space*

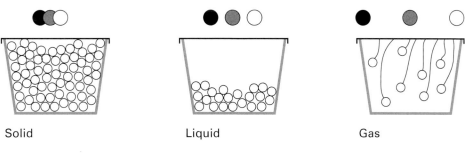

Solid   Liquid   Gas

4.8 *Beads as solid, liquid and gas*

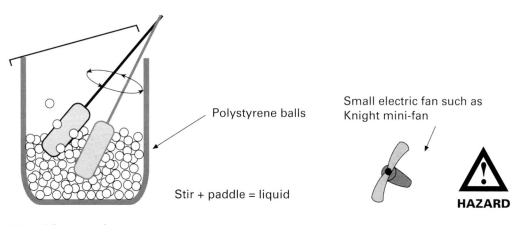

Polystyrene balls

Stir + paddle = liquid

Small electric fan such as
Knight mini-fan

HAZARD

4.9 *Material state and energy*

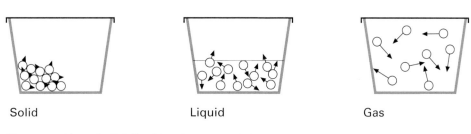

Solid   Liquid   Gas

4.10 *Representation of solid, liquid and gaseous state*

3 Drama – children represent particles of water frozen into solid ice (static, holding onto each other); melting into liquid water (moving around slowly, near each other) and evaporating into water vapour particles (free movement around the room) (Figure **4.11**).

Conventional representation
Representation usually shows particles as small round objects and arrows indicating the direction and energy of movement (Figure **4.10**).

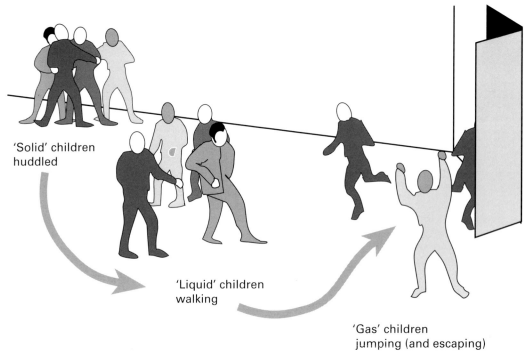

'Solid' children
huddled

'Liquid' children
walking

'Gas' children
jumping (and escaping)

4.11 *The solid/liquid/gas drama*

Points to make clear

❑ In Figure **4.2**, the ice and water in the balloons are the same 'material' – but not the air in the third balloon. (It would need to be full of water vapour.)

❑ In Figure **4.3**, the full explanation would involve a consideration of the pressure of the air outside on the inflated and deflated balloons. The simplest explanation is that the air in the inflated balloon is compressed, that is, denser than the air in the deflated balloon and this 'extra air' causes the difference in mass.

❑ Some liquids change into gases at room temperature without additional heating. The Olbas oil and perfume are both liquid and gas – we can see the liquid and smell the gas. Eventually these liquids would evaporate completely at room temperature.

❑ Refer to specific gases in air sometimes, not just 'the air'.

❑ Helium balloons deflate because helium leaks out and air gases leak in – gases do move around a lot! The balloon will come down because the helium (very lightweight gas particles) has been replaced by the heavier air gases. A helium balloon kept overnight will demonstrate this quite well.

❑ Carbon dioxide is heavier than other air gases (see the milk bottle experiment above and the candle experiment below).

HAZARD

❑ Not all colourless, odourless liquids are water or drinkable (e.g. white spirit, vodka, etc.). *Children should never taste liquids without an adult's permission.*

❑ In Figures **4.8** and **4.10**, the distances between the particles are exaggerated to make the point. The scientific view is that water behaves unlike other liquids as water molecules are 'further apart' in the solid (ice) than in the liquid (as water). In the drama (**4.11**) talk about the empty space or 'nothing' between the children, which helps to explain compressibility. Children may suggest that there is 'air' in the spaces between the actual molecules – 'nothing' is a very difficult concept to grasp! No single analogy or illustration is sufficient to deal with all children's misconceptions.

4.2 Mixtures

National Curriculum reference
Sc3 Materials and their properties
Pupils should be taught:
KS2   2a to describe changes that occur when materials are mixed
       3a how to separate solid particles of different sizes by sieving
       3e to use knowledge of solids, liquids and gases to decide how mixtures
           might be separated

Scottish National Guidelines
Environmental Studies. Changing materials
Level B   describe how materials can be changed by heating and cooling
Level C   describe the changes when materials are mixed
          describe how solids of different sizes can be separated

Relevant QCA unit
4D   Solids, liquids and how they can be separated

What's the problem?

■ Identifying a mixture – we can't always see the different substances it contains, e.g. icing sugar, cocoa powder, tinned tomatoes (read the list of ingredients).

What might children think?

Children are likely to:

❑ think that air is a single gas, rather than a mixture of gases

❑ equate 'pure' with 'clean, beautiful, bright' rather than a single substance

❑ think that the solute has simply 'disappeared'.

The challenge for the teacher

The teacher needs to convince children that:

❑ air is a mixture of gases

❑ a solution is a mixture of two substances that can be separated

❑ other substances (e.g. soil) may not look like mixtures but they are

❑ the properties of the mixture are dependent on the different components of the
    mixture (e.g. watering plants with salty/fresh water; different cake mixtures).

Vocabulary issues

'Pure' may be thought of as a single substance; 'dissolving' is sometimes confused with 'melting'; words like: mixture, solution, solute; solvent may equate with toxic; 'disappeared' into the liquid suggests no substance, no weight.

Possible starting points

1 Identify and discuss everyday uses of the words 'mixed' and 'mixtures' and what they mean (cake mix, mixed spice, Dolly Mixture, mixed fruit, mixed vegetable etc.).

2 Predict and discuss the effects of mixing separate ingredients and the changes after cooking.

3 Read food packaging and discuss the listed ingredients and additives.

Focus ## Mixtures of solids can be separated

1 Explore ways to separate solid mixtures. Use separation techniques such as: DIY and commercial sieves (Figure **4.12**); adding water, then filtering (filter papers or coffee filters) and evaporating (windowsill or radiator); using magnets. (Children can be asked to speculate about the environmental source of the mixtures.)

Suggested mixtures:
- ❏ **classroom** – pencils, pencil sharpeners, erasers, etc.
- ❏ **kitchen** – dried peas, flour, salt, paprika, muesli, dried soup mixture, etc.
- ❏ **seaside** (made up for safety) – sand, shells, pebbles, pieces of 'driftwood', small blunt (magnetic) nails, sea salt crystals, perhaps clean 'litter' – crisp packets, milk bottle tops, etc.
- ❏ **metals** – springs, metal weights, washers, drinks cans, different nails, coins, etc.
- ❏ **garden** – school garden soil.

CARE – *wash hands after handling, teachers may need to supervise to ensure that this is done properly.*

Note: the more items and the more separation techniques you include, the greater the need for children to have skills and prior knowledge. Separating mixtures also gives the opportunity to use and refer appropriately to scientific apparatus, e.g. funnel, filter paper, sieve.

Focus ## Some liquids mix together, others do not

1 Predict what will happen when liquids begin to mix. Pour one slowly over the surface of the other, observe, then stir.

Suggested mixtures (including some immiscible liquids):
- ❏ concentrated blackcurrant juice to water
- ❏ vegetable oil to water (or coloured water)
- ❏ golden syrup into water and water into golden syrup (stir well!)
- ❏ marbling inks to water
- ❏ warm coloured water to cold, very salty water.

Currents occur when (warm) fresh river water meets with salty sea water, and they begin to mix together.
TAKE CARE *when swimming in these areas. In the same way, different densities of air will cause air currents and turbulence.*

Focus ## Air is a mixture of gases

1 Illustrate and discuss burning. Put a candle into a dish floating in a container of water and light it (Figure **4.13**). Invert a jam jar over the candle so that there is clearance for the flame. Predict what will happen when the candle burns inside the jar. Encourage all explanations – combustion and gas exchange is a complex procedure and it is unlikely that children will understand the whole process from one experience.

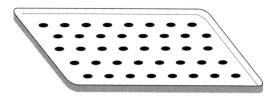

Polystyrene tray with holes

Cup with holes

4.12 *Sieves*

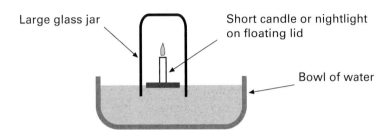

Large glass jar

Short candle or nightlight on floating lid

Bowl of water

4.13 *What is in air – the candle experiment*

Points to make clear

❏ The flame goes out in the above illustration because (a) combustion uses some of the oxygen in the air, (b) carbon dioxide is produced which does not support combustion and (c) carbon dioxide is a heavy gas and gradually fills the lower half of the jam jar. The water level will go up, partly because of the change in gas volumes, partly because some of the carbon dioxide dissolves in the water. The space above the candle indicates that there are some gases left (including some oxygen gas and others, mainly nitrogen).

❏ Although vigorous stirring appears to mix some immiscible liquids (e.g. oil and water) the oil particles are suspended in the water, not dissolved.

Use of ideas, applications and extensions

❏ What is happening when we whisk (mix) air into egg-whites?

❏ What is smoke and why is it dangerous?

❏ What's inside a tea/herbal tea bag? What comes out in water and why?

❏ What's in a milk shake? What's in candy floss? What's in a powdered soup mix?

❏ What is a bubble made of?

❏ Is a football solid?

❏ What's inside a cake?

❏ What's inside an aerosol spray? (Try to obtain a transparent aerosol can to look inside and read the ingredients.)

❏ Set up a debate on the use of additives in food mixtures (preservatives, colourings, artificial flavourings) for food storage and persuasive marketing.

4.3 Dissolving gases & solids in liquids

National Curriculum reference
Sc3 Materials and their properties
Pupils should be taught:
KS2	**2a**	to describe the changes that occur when materials are mixed
	2d	about reversible changes, including dissolving and evaporating
	3b	that some solids dissolve in water but some do not
	3e	to use knowledge of solids, liquids and gases to decide how mixtures might be separated

Scottish National Guidelines
Environmental studies. Changing materials
Level C distinguish between soluble and insoluble materials; describe in simple terms the changes that occur when water is heated or cooled

Relevant QCA unit
6C	More about dissolving
6D	Reversible and irreversible changes

What's the problem?

■ Learning to think about where the bubbles come from in a fizzy drink.

■ Asking where the sugar goes when we stir it in our tea: what is happening to make the stuff disappear and how it is we can get the stuff back again.

■ Recognising that matter can be changed but is always 'there' – it must be accounted for.

What might children think?

Children are likely to:

❏ focus on the solid solute only – they say 'it just goes', 'it disappears', 'it melts away', 'it dissolves away', 'it turns into water'

❏ confuse melting with dissolving – both go runny

❏ believe that the dissolved solute has no weight. The sugar is 'up in the water', 'suspended in the water' so does not increase the weight of the solution.

❏ in gaseous solutions, gases 'don't weigh anything' so fizzy drinks, with or without the gas in them, weigh the same.

Vocabulary issues

'Dissolved' may be equated with melting and everyday metaphors ('dissolved/melted into thin air'); 'disappeared' equated with weightless, no substance; 'solution' equated with the answer to a problem; 'solvent' associated with 'solvent abuse'; 'suspension' associated with 'suspended' from school; other terms that confuse include evaporate, dry out, solute.

4.14 *Concept cartoon – the lemonade problem*

reduced, from Keogh and Naylor, *Concept Cartoons in Science Education*, 2000

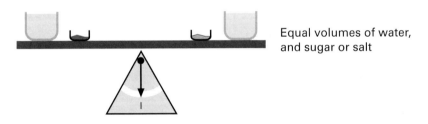

Equal volumes of water, and sugar or salt

4.15 *The balance problem (in solution!)*

The challenge for the teacher

The teacher needs to convince children that:

❑ the solute is still there, although invisible

❑ the solution is the combined weight of the solvent AND the solute

❑ if the solvent is evaporated, we can get a solid solute back again: a reversible change (we would not get a dissolved gas back).

Possible starting point

1 Think about what happens to sugar in tea. Is it still there? How do we know? Could we get it back?

2 Use the concept cartoon on fizzy drinks (Figure **4.14**) and a bottle of fizzy lemonade for discussion and possible explanations. (Children may suggest that 'the bottle will lose gas and weigh the same ... or less'; 'the air coming in will balance the gas going out so the weight stays the same'; 'the weight of the gases is so little you can't measure it', etc.)

Focus | # The solute is still there when in solution

1 Illustrate and discuss dissolving. Set up a beam balance with transparent containers of equal volumes of water and small cups of identical masses of sugar or salt on each side, such that the beam is balanced. Discuss what might occur if the sugar is dissolved on one side only (Figure **4.15**).

2 Show differences in solutions. Fill two transparent containers (water tanks or large jars) – one with tap water, the other with salt water. The two will look the same but will show differences when used in investigations. For example, ask the children to predict, compare and discuss objects that might float, sink, only just float and only just sink in the two liquids (a collection of fruits is good for this) (Figure **4.16**).

3 Discuss what swimming might be like in the Dead Sea (very, very salty water) compared with swimming in freshwater (e.g. the local pool) or the sea around our coast. Ask why chlorine-based disinfectants are dissolved in the swimming-pool water.

4 Demonstrate recovering the solute by evaporating a salt solution to dryness (*see* section **4.4**, page 37).

5 Dissolve coloured solutes (e.g. Oxo cubes, jelly crystals, instant coffee) in water.

6 Illustrate the different solutes in water-based felt tip pens, food colourings and inks in a chromatography activity. Use jars, filter paper (or white coffee filters), water and pipettes (Figure **4.17**).

7 Demonstrate separation. Separate the solids from milk by pouring a bottle of full cream or Jersey cream milk into a hygienic bowl and add the juice from a whole lemon. Strain/filter the results through a sterile cloth (e.g. clean muslin) and discuss the outcome of curds and whey (Figure **4.18**). (A tasty curd cheese can be made by adding a little salt and herbs (e.g. chives) to the curds, compacting this and spreading on dry biscuits. Asian families often use curds and whey in traditional home recipes.)

CARE – if food is to be tasted, it is important to follow good hygiene procedures.

Focus | # In a solution, neither the solute nor the solvent are physically changed

Representing solute and solution

1 Fill a transparent yogurt pot with dried lentils. Discuss any differences or changes after stirring in currants, raisins or sultanas (Oversby [1]) (Figure **4.19**).

2 Fill a shallow dish such that the wooden beads or broad beans go up to the edge. Predict what will happen if you add some rice to the dish, then some more, and some more.

3 Demonstrate what happens in the same dish when you fill it with marbles, then add sand, then add water. Discuss how you might recover each ingredient.

4 Discuss what happens if we go on adding salt to the water, e.g. 'Will it always go on dissolving?' 'If not, why not?'
At a certain point no more salt can be dissolved in the water – the solution becomes saturated.

5 Dramatise the solvent and solute with movement as follows:

Sugar in tea: some children link arms together as the solvent, other children as the solute squeeze in between the solvent particles.

Fizzy drink: some children are the slow-moving liquid particles, others the fast-moving gas particles.
This gives the opportunity to discuss why the gas doesn't 'escape'; fizzy drinks are bottled under pressure, releasing the lid releases the pressure allowing gases to escape from the liquid, and air gases to come in.

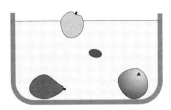

Tap water in bowl
with fruit such as apple, pomegranate
grape and pear

Salt water in bowl

4.16 *Floating fruit in different liquids*

Water based ink on centre
of filter paper and placed
on beaker

Water dropped
on ink (slowly)

Water based ink at base of T-bar
filter paper suspended in beaker

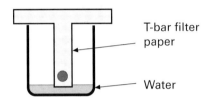

T-bar filter
paper

Water

4.17 *Chromatography*

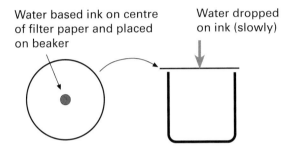

Milk

Juice of one lemon

Folded new J-cloth

Curds

Whey

4.18 *Filtration apparatus, curds and whey*

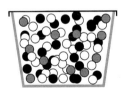

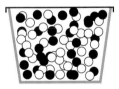

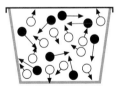

4.19 *Mixture*

4.20 *Conventional representations*

Conventional representation

Solutions are usually represented by round particles of solvent with round particles of
solute in between them (Figure **4.20**).

Points to make clear

❏ Particles are not necessarily round in shape.

❏ Solvents are not always water, e.g. white spirit is used for some marbling paints, and need to be treated with caution.

❏ We can separate a non-soluble solid from a liquid by filtering, which is like sieving.

❏ We cannot separate out a dissolved solid from a solution by using a sieve or a filter as we might separate different beads. The particles are too small. We have to evaporate the solvent to recover the solute – this is an example of a reversible change.

❏ There aren't big spaces between the water particles ... and sugar particles are actually larger than water particles.

Use of ideas, applications and extensions

❏ If fish and other marine life live on oxygen gas, where do they get their oxygen from and how?

❏ What happens to the oxygen gas we breathe in?

❏ What happens if we try to dissolve paprika ... or flour ... or powder paints?

The particles are held in the liquids in a cloudy 'suspension' – they do not dissolve. Eventually these particles sink to the bottom. Even smaller particles, such as in milk, form a 'colloidal suspension' and do not sink however long they are left.

4.4 Evaporation and condensation

National Curriculum reference
Sc3 Materials and their properties
Pupils should be taught:

KS1   **2b** to explore and describe the way some everyday materials ... change
            when they are heated or cooled

KS2   **2d** about reversible changes, including ... evaporation
            2e the part played by evaporation (and condensation) in the water cycle
            3d how to recover dissolved solids by evaporating the liquid from solution

Scottish National Guidelines
Environmental studies. Changing materials

Level C   describe in simple terms the changes that occur when water is heated or
              cooled

Level D   explain how evaporation and filtration can be used in the separation of
              solids from liquids

Relevant QCA unit
4D   Solids and liquids: how they can be separated

What's the problem?

■ Where does the stuff go to?

What might children think?

Younger children may accept the disappearance of water without offering any
explanation. Older children are likely to suggest that water:

❏ has leaked out somehow

❏ has been drunk, taken, or mopped up by a person or animal

❏ goes 'somewhere'

❏ disappears into 'thin air'

❏ gets sucked up by the Sun or the clouds.

In some of these cases, it appears that children think of the air, Sun or clouds as
receptacles to hold the evaporated water. Evaporation also seems to be associated with
absorption; the 'milk dries up into the breakfast cereal' (Driver *et al.* [2] and Russell *et al.*,
[3]) and 'the water on the paper towel *dries up* by *going into* the paper towel' (Wright and
Wiggins [4]).

Children may not believe that we can 'get the water back again'. Children may believe
that the evaporated liquid becomes weightless. Children sometimes describe the reverse
change, condensation, as 'the coldness changing into water' or as occurring when 'warm
meets cold'. Children appear to believe that cold water or ice can diffuse through
somehow.

The challenge for the teacher

The teacher needs to convince children that:

❑ the water or other liquid is still there in another state

❑ the water vapour can always (in principle) be recovered as liquid water

❑ the water vapour has the same mass as the liquid water.

Vocabulary issues

'Disappeared' suggests no longer existing, weightless; evaporate is equated with sucked up; dried up with absorbed. We have 'evaporated' and 'condensed' milk. Condensation is often seen as 'the mist on the window' rather than the process.

Possible starting points

1 Put water into a tank, a glass and/or a dish. Mark the levels, leave overnight and discuss any changes observed then and later. Repeat by leaving the containers on a sunny windowsill or in a warm place.

2 Make puddles on the playground – predict, observe changes, record (e.g. drawing) and discuss changes. (Puddles will not only 'disappear' by evaporating but will partly be absorbed by ground materials (stone, tarmac) depending on the surface on which they form.)

3 Compare water levels in two tanks of water over several days, one with cling film (or similar) over it, one without. Discuss what happens to the underside of the cling film.

Focus ## Water changes when it is heated and cooled

1 Show evaporation. Boil a kettle (safely) in the classroom and observe the effects.

2 Discuss what happens to moisture in the air. Use an atomiser or clean plant spray to spray water droplets into the air (Figure **4.21**).

3 Demonstrate evaporation and condensation. Put a transparent plastic cup at the bottom of an airtight transparent food bag. Pour in a little water and use the twists to fasten the bag tightly, leaving a space over the cup. Weigh the bag + cup and leave in a very warm place. Observe and discuss the changes. If possible, try weighing the package when some or all of the water has evaporated. Eventually some of the condensation begins to form droplets of water and run down the side of the bag. Alternatively, predict and discuss what happens if the covered cup is left in a very cold place for a few hours. This can also be tried with coloured water or salty water (Figure **4.22**).

Focus ## Liquid water can change into water vapour (gas) and change back again

1 Use drama to represent the change (*see* pages 27, 28). Discuss where the energy comes from for the water particles to move around more freely.

2 Discuss the concept cartoon on condensation (Figure **4.23**).

You may have to accept that many children will cling to their existing ideas until they have sufficient evidence to convince them of an alternative explanation. Sometimes, children will hold BOTH explanations simultaneously.

4.21 *Plant spray atomiser*

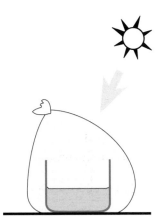

4.22 *Evaporation*

4.23 *Ideas about condensation*

reduced, from Keogh and Naylor, *Concept Cartoons in Science Education*, 2000

Points to make clear

❏ Things that 'disappear' can be 'still there' but not visible to our eyes (like germs or bacteria in some old foods).

❏ Evaporation takes place at ordinary room or outdoor temperatures, at all temperatures; it is NOT necessary to boil water. Increased heat and boiling simply accelerate the rate of evaporation. If electric kettles did not have an automatic cut-off switch at the boiling point, all the water would evaporate and the kettle element would burn out (as often happened in the past).

5 Forces

5.1 The force of friction

National Curriculum reference
Sc4 Physical processes
Pupils should be taught:
KS2   **2c** about friction, including air resistance, as a force that slows moving
objects and may prevent objects from starting to move

Scottish National Guidelines
Environmental studies. Forces and their effects
Level C   give some examples of friction
explain friction in simple terms
describe air resistance in terms of friction

Relevant QCA unit
4E   Friction

What's the problem?

■ Learning to think about the movement of objects in terms of forces rather than actions, e.g. children know that a ball can be made to move by kicking it, throwing it or hitting it with a bat but need to recognise that the action does not matter – in all cases the ball moves because of a force.

■ Moving from knowing what happens to thinking about explanations, e.g. children know that objects slide better on smooth surfaces, but need to learn to think about this in terms of decreased friction.

■ Developing a conceptual model in which objects are 'seen' to be subject to forces of various kinds, e.g. the movement of a sheet of paper falling through the air is affected by the forces of gravity and air resistance.

■ Imagining forces produced by inanimate, non-moving objects, e.g. a wall exerting a force on a person leaning against it.

What might children think?

Children are likely to:

❏ know from experience that when they push things, such as wheeled toys, they move and then stop, but are likely to think this is because the 'push' runs out

❏ know that a bigger push makes something travel further

❏ know that things stop more quickly on rough surfaces

❏ know that it is harder to move things on rough surfaces (e.g. it is harder to pedal a bike on rough ground than smooth concrete)

❏ know that some things grip well and some slide easily (e.g. when you want to go fast down a slide)

❏ have heard of friction but equate it with the action of rubbing

❏ explain changes in the movement of objects in terms of actions, rather than forces.

The challenge for the teacher

The teacher needs to:

❑ draw on children's experience of moving and stationary objects and to raise questions about things which are taken for granted, such as why a toy pushed across the floor slows down and stops

❑ support children in developing the ability to think about objects in terms of the forces acting on them, especially when those forces are not produced by an obvious push or pull

❑ develop a line of reasoning which can be used in many situations, including those in which the forces are not obvious, e.g. when the motion of an object is changing in some way, the forces on it are not balanced

❑ make 'invisible' forces imaginable, e.g. by using analogies

❑ make links between related contexts and examples.

Vocabulary issues

By the time children come to think about friction, they should be aware of the scientific use of the word 'force'. Nevertheless, everyday uses, often related to the verb associated with 'making things happen' – being forced to go to bed, forcing a door open, etc., still affect children's thinking, but can be used to advantage.

Children may confuse friction with other words used in school, such as fiction or fraction.

Friction may be thought of as synonymous with 'rubbing'. It is commonly associated with 'friction burns' from sliding down ropes.

Possible starting points

Before starting to consider 'invisible' forces, where there appears to be nothing actively pushing or pulling, children need to be confident about situations in which obvious forces stop or slow down objects. Not only do they need to know what happens, they also need to be able to identify the force and the direction in which it is acting.

1 Ask children to mime, act out or imagine situations where a moving object is slowed down or stopped by someone. Useful examples might include someone:
   ❑ holding back a dog by pulling on its lead
   ❑ holding on to a person to stop them from running away
   ❑ pulling back on the handle of a pram or shopping trolley when it starts to speed up going down a slope.

Emphasise that, in each case, the person slows down the moving object by pulling in the direction opposite to the direction of movement. Without such a force, the dog, person, pram or trolley would keep on going.

2 Ask children to mime, act out or imagine situations where a moving person is slowed down or stopped by something. Useful examples here might include:
   ❑ walking into a strong wind
   ❑ running down a sandy beach and then into the sea.

Again, emphasise that the person is slowed down by a force in the opposite direction to the movement.

In discussion, focus on the need for a 'slowing-down force' only. An important misconception is that moving objects need a force to keep them moving. In the examples above there is a force keeping the objects moving, generated by the dog, the person or gravity. However, this is not relevant to the explanation which needs to be developed, which is about how things that are already moving can be slowed down or stopped.

Use children's knowledge of going down slides (polished, dirty, wearing jeans, with bare legs) to focus attention on the fact that some surfaces (usually rougher ones) slow things down more than others. Emphasise that surfaces can affect movement.

direction of movement of top egg box

push-back of bottom egg box

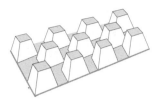

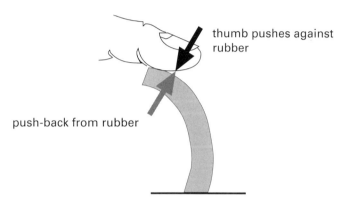

5.1   *The egg box model of friction*

thumb pushes against rubber

push-back from rubber

5.2   *The force produced by bending a rubber*

Focus   **Friction is a force which slows down moving objects**

1   Give a box, or a wooden block, a push, so it slides across the floor. Build up a line of reasoning which is something like:

❏ we know that moving things need a force to slow them down or stop them.
❏ when a box/wooden block slows down as it slides across the floor there must be a force causing this to happen.
❏ as we can't see anything pushing or pulling, what could be causing the force?
❏ when the box moves over the floor, this must produce a force.
❏ we know that surfaces can affect how quickly things slow down/stop so the surface must affect the size of the force.
❏ this force is called friction and it slows the box down and eventually stops it.

2   Make this plausible by providing a way of imagining how a surface, such as the floor, can produce a force, for example:

❏ feeling the force between surfaces: pushing hands together and trying to move one over the other allows the force to be felt. Repeating this with a small amount of cooking oil between the hands allows the effect of the use of lubricants to be demonstrated.
❏ use hand lenses to look at surfaces. Notice that even surfaces which appear very smooth are, under magnification, actually bumpy.
❏ use egg boxes (or some foam packaging materials) to demonstrate how bumps on surfaces can interlock and make it difficult for the surfaces to slide over each other (Figure **5.1**). The egg boxes represent a magnified view of two surfaces.
❏ use a long rubber to demonstrate how protrusions, such as those on egg boxes, produce a force when deformed. When one end of the rubber is bent, the rubber can be felt pushing back (Figure **5.2**).

❏ Use two hairbrushes to model what happens when one surface moves across another. As the top brush is pushed, the bristles can be seen to push against each other. As each bristle is bent it pushes back in the opposite direction, generating a force against the direction of movement (Figure **5.3**).

Points to make clear

❏ Friction is caused by the interaction of two surfaces. The combination of materials is important.

❏ Whenever two surfaces move over one another there is a force, friction, which acts against the movement. The size of this force depends on the surfaces.

❏ Children's thinking about 'something' being 'used up' as a moving object slows and stops is more in line with an explanation in terms of energy. When an object is given a push along a horizontal surface, energy is transferred to it (by the pusher). As the object moves energy is lost, due to friction, as heat. When all the energy has been transferred, the object stops. The force enables energy to be transferred.

Examples that link friction as a force and friction producing heat include: rubbing hands together, rubbing sticks together to make fire, striking matches, etc.

Use of ideas, applications and extensions

Children could use the idea of friction:

1 To carry out or develop investigations:

❏ Order a range of surfaces in terms of the frictional force produced. The material of one surface must be kept constant, e.g. use different 'supporting' surfaces such as a wooden floor, carpet or concrete and keep the surface of the sliding object the same; or keep the 'supporting' surface the same and change the surface which slides over it – by using a block with surfaces of sandpaper, hardboard, plastic, etc.

❏ Find which combination of surfaces produces the greatest, and least, force of friction, using say three or four different surfaces in combination.

❏ Does mass affect friction? (increasing the mass increases friction).

❏ Does surface area affect friction between solid surfaces? (increasing surface area does not increase friction).

❏ Find out how friction between two surfaces can be increased or reduced.

2 In thought experiments:

❏ If we could make a perfectly smooth surface, what would happen to an object sliding across it? (If the surface were completely smooth there would be no friction – if we discount air resistance – so the object would continue moving for ever.)

❏ If an object were pushed out of a spaceship, what would happen to it? (Since there is nothing to rub against the surface of the object there would be no friction and it would continue moving at the same speed – until affected by another force such as the gravity of a star.)

❏ If friction could be 'switched off' what do you think would happen?

3 To explain everyday uses:

❏ Why do goalkeepers wear rough gloves?

❏ How do the brakes on bicycles work?

❏ Why do engines need oil?

❏ When is friction useful?

❏ When is friction a nuisance?

Note that 'grips' on shoes can be a distraction (they are only effective on rough surfaces) – but they can also illustrate the source of the frictional force.

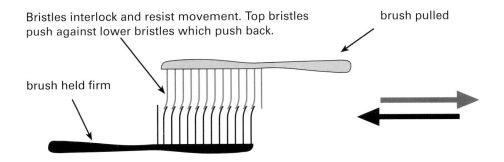

Bristles interlock and resist movement. Top bristles push against lower bristles which push back.

brush pulled

brush held firm

5.3 *The hairbrush model*

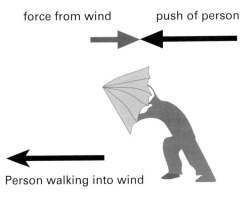

force from wind

push of person

Person walking into wind

5.4 *Air resistance*

4 Using the 'interlocking' model, to explain experimental results:
   ❏ Why does friction increase with mass? (the protrusions are pushed together more)
   ❏ Why does friction not increase with surface area? (as the surface area increases, the force is spread over a greater area, i.e. a greater number of protrusions. However, the protrusions are pushed together less than when the surface area is small.)

NOTE: the teacher needs to consider whether it is likely to be easier to deal with static or dynamic friction, and, probably, to deal initially with one of these only.

Static friction is the force which prevents things from starting to move, even when a force is applied. In this case, the force of friction must be exactly equivalent to the push or pull acting to move the object.

Dynamic friction is the frictional force acting against a moving object. It is likely that this will be easier to deal with in terms of constructing an argument.

To get an object to move (i.e. to accelerate it) requires more force than to keep it moving at a constant speed. This can cause some difficulties in investigations. Teachers will need to be clear which of these they want children to measure, and whether the practical set up allows this to be done easily.

Focus **Air and water resistance**

1 Talk with children about situations in which they can feel air or water pushing against them, e.g. when walking against the wind, running with an umbrella, or swimming. Emphasise that they are pushing against the air/water and it is pushing back.

2 Represent such situations by diagrams or drawings with arrows to indicate the forces and think about the relative size of the forces (see Figure **5.4**).

5.5 *Air resistance to a flat sheet of paper and a crumpled ball of paper*

Points to make clear

❏ Air resistance and water resistance can be thought of as frictional forces, caused by 'rubbing' when an object moves through them. Thinking of objects 'pushing through' water or air may provide a useful introduction to ideas about friction as a force opposing motion, since children can relate to a first-hand experience.

❏ In most classroom situations, the force of air resistance is so small that we can ignore it.

Use of ideas, applications and extensions

1 Explore what affects the size of the resisting force, e.g.:

❏ Drop flat and screwed-up sheets of paper and compare how long they take to fall to the ground (Figure **5.5**)

❏ Move sheets of card or polystyrene through air. How do size and orientation of the sheet affect the force needed?

❏ Move your hand through water. What difference does it make if your fingers are together or apart? What if your hand is in a plastic bag?

❏ Do all liquids give the same resistance? What happens if you drop a marble into a tall cylinder of water? a tall cylinder of golden syrup?

2 Think about situations in which air resistance is useful (e.g. parachutes, seed dispersal, meteors burning up in the Earth's atmosphere). How does it affect movement? What other forces are involved?

3 Think about situations in which air resistance needs to be reduced (design of cars, cycling, projectiles, etc). How is it reduced? What other forces are involved?

4 Find examples in which animals control the effects of air or water resistance, e.g. the way ducks move their feet when paddling, humans move when swimming, birds use their wings to glide or dive etc.

5 Make links to upthrust, floating and sinking, and streamlining.

6 Electricity

6.1 Simple circuits

National Curriculum reference
Sc 4 Physical processes
Pupils should be taught:
KS1   **1a** about everyday appliances that use electricity
          1b about simple series circuits involving batteries, wires, bulbs and other components
          1c how a switch can be used to break a circuit.
KS2   **1a** to construct simple circuits, incorporating a battery or power supply and a range of switches to make electrical devices work
          1b how changing the number or type of components in a series circuit can make bulbs brighter or dimmer
          1c how to represent series circuits by drawings and conventional symbols and how to construct series circuits on the basis of drawings and diagrams using conventional symbols.

Scottish National Guidelines
Environmental studies. Properties and uses of energy; Conversion and transfer of energy
Level C construct simple battery-operated circuits, identifying the main components
            describe the energy conversions in the components of an electrical circuit
Level E use the terms 'voltage', 'current' and 'resistance' in the context of simple circuits

Relevant QCA units
2F   Using electricity
4F   Circuits and conductors
6G   Changing circuits

What's the problem?

■ 'Electricity' is not visible, though its effects are.

■ From experience with circuits children will develop their own explanations for what they observe. These are unlikely to agree with the scientific explanation.

■ Developing a more scientific explanation involves learning to use a specific vocabulary related to ideas such as current, voltage and resistance, which cannot be seen.

What might children think?

Children are likely to:

❏ learn quickly how to make circuits, and connect up different components, but see the purpose of this as 'getting the bulb to light'

❏ know that batteries are needed to make circuits work, and think that this is because they contain electricity which they supply to the circuit. They are likely to think of electricity as some kind of substance supplied to a house, like a gas.

❏ know that batteries 'go flat' and think that this is because they have used up all their electricity. They may think that flat batteries are lighter than new ones.

❏ learn that two wires are needed to make a circuit unless the battery and the component are touching, but explain this by saying that the second wire is 'for safety' or because one wire cannot carry enough electricity. Household electrical appliances appear to be connected to the supply by one 'wire' and not be part of a circuit.

❏ think that electricity flows out of both battery terminals to the component

❏ attach great significance to the positive and negative signs on the battery and may think they produce different 'kinds' of electricity

❏ learn that electricity flows along a circular path but think that it gets used up in the circuit, so that less returns to the battery than leaves it. They may also think that the second bulb in a circuit will shine less brightly than the first because the first has 'used up some of the electricity'.

Underlying much of children's thinking about electricity is a 'source-consumer' model in which the battery supplies something to the bulb. Some typical ways of thinking about circuits are summarised in Figure 6.1.

The challenge for the teacher

The teacher needs to:

❏ recognise which ideas can be challenged by practical experience and which cannot

❏ know how to make specific teaching interventions to introduce ideas and be able to relate them to practical experience.

Possible starting points

Initially children need to develop competence and confidence in making circuits for themselves. They then need to be helped to recognise that a circuit is a continuous pathway and that 'electricity' travels *through* the bulb not *to* the bulb (and also through the battery).

1 Focus children's attention on the connections to the bulb and the battery when no holders for the bulb or battery are used. How many different connections are possible? Which combinations make the bulb light/not light?

2 Use large, clear bulbs, pictures, or hand lenses, so that children can see the internal structure of a bulb. Notice the filament and how it is connected to the casing (Figure 6.2) and emphasise the idea of a continuous pathway.

3 Use children's familiarity with the word 'circuit' in other contexts to develop the idea of a continuous pathway, e.g. in motor racing, a circuit is the path the cars travel along. They may pass through the pits, or tunnels, on the way. In circuit training, people move from one activity to the next in a sequence and return to the start point.

4 Challenge children's thinking:

❏ are household electrical leads really just one wire?

❏ if the second wire is needed because not enough electricity can get along one wire, would a thicker wire make a difference? Or two wires connected to the same terminals?

5 Support the idea of a 'one-way flow' by thinking about the behaviour of bulbs, buzzers and motors in a circuit when the connections to the battery are reversed. (There will be no effect on the bulb, the motor will reverse its direction of spin and the buzzer will usually not work.)

Thinking about 'electricity' going 'all the way round and back' raises a problem. If the 'electricity' comes back, why does the battery go flat? A logical explanation would be that 'less' comes back, and this leads to a major and persistent misconception. It is at this point that the ideas of current and energy need to be separated.

'Unipolar' model:
only one wire is needed

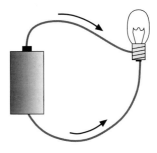

'Clashing currents' model:
electricity travels along both wires to
the bulb.

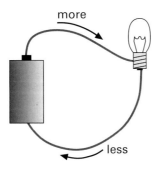

'Consumption' or 'reduction' model:
current gets used up in the circuit.

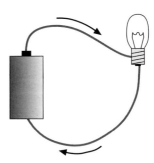

'Scientific' model:
current is constant at all parts of the
circuit

6.1   *Typical ways of thinking about simple series circuits*

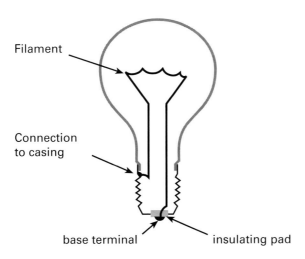

6.2   *Diagram of light bulb showing electrical path between light bulb casing, filament and
base terminal*

Focus **Explaining how a circuit works**

Practical exploration can allow children to find out what happens when, for example, an additional (identical) bulb is added to a circuit in series with the first. The bulbs are equally bright, but dimmer than one bulb alone. In order to begin to explain how this happens, we have to imagine what is going on 'inside the wires' and to differentiate the concept of electricity into two separate ideas, current and energy.

There are many analogies which can be used to support this, all of which have strengths and weaknesses. The 'soap-dispenser' model used in Section **3.1** *The heart and circulation* was originally designed to represent a simple circuit (see Figure **3.2**).

Four examples of analogies which can be used in relation to circuits are:

A1   The bicycle chain

Representation of the physical circuit

Battery represented by the person on the bicycle.

Wires have no physical representation.

Bulb represented by the bicycle wheel.

Representation of current and energy

Current represented by moving chain.

Energy has no physical representation.

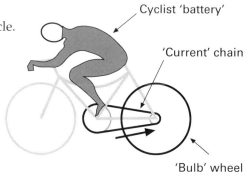

Cyclist 'battery'

'Current' chain

'Bulb' wheel

Points to make clear

About current

❏ The whole chain starts and stops moving at the same time.

❏ The chain does not get used up.

❏ The current (chain) is needed to carry energy to the wheel.

About energy

❏ Energy is transferred from the person pedalling to the wheels by the chain.

A2   'Smartie' children

Representation of the physical circuit

Battery represented by container of Smarties.

Wires represented by path taken by children.
This needs to be marked out in some way, for example a chalked pathway.

Bulb represented by an obstacle which has to be climbed over, under or through and so demands some effort.

Representation of current and energy

Current represented by moving children.

Energy represented by Smartie.

Points to make clear

About current

❏ When all the Smarties have been used up, no current can flow anywhere as the battery cannot provide the 'push'.

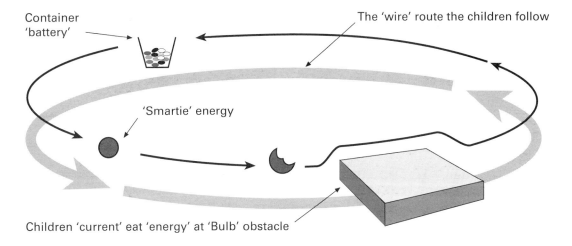

Container 'battery'

The 'wire' route the children follow

'Smartie' energy

Children 'current' eat 'energy' at 'Bulb' obstacle

About energy

❑ Link the analogy to children's intuitive notions of food, particularly sweet things, providing energy needed to do something.

❑ Stress that it is easy to move along the chalked route but that to get through the obstacle requires energy, which is provided by the Smartie.

❑ When there are no Smarties left in the dish, this represents a flat battery which has transferred all its energy.

Disadvantages and limitations

❑ It can be difficult to keep children evenly spaced around the circuit. This can make the idea that the current is the same in all parts of the circuit difficult to represent clearly.

❑ At the start, children 'before' the obstacle need to have a Smartie, but those after it do not.

❑ The children still 'contain' the Smartie, after the obstacle. Therefore it is necessary to stress that the Smartie provides just enough energy to get over/through the obstacle.

❑ The 'push' of the battery is not represented unless children are given a little push as they receive their Smartie.

Variations on the idea

Children (current) travel along a route carrying balls (energy) from a basket (battery) to a chute/container (bulb) and back to the basket. The balls need to 'do something', for example, make a noise in the container, or be carried away along a chute. The disadvantage of this is that, unlike energy, the balls collect at the 'bulb'.

A3   Firebuckets and other 'carrier' models

Children stand in a circle which includes a bucket of water opposite a sink with a water wheel or similar device. Each child has a paper cup in their left hand. Those cups clockwise from the full bucket should be half full of water at the start. On a given signal everyone passes their cup, simultaneously, to the person on their left and receives a new cup in their right hand. The child nearest the full bucket refills each cup as it comes to him or her. The child nearest the sink pours the water away, making the water wheel spin. The secret of making this analogy work is in keeping a rhythm going so that everyone passes their cups at the same time, maintaining a constant flow.

Representation of the physical circuit

Battery represented by bucket of water.

Wires represented by children, standing in a circle.

Bulb represented by water wheel in sink.

Representation of current and energy

Current represented by moving cups.

Energy represented by water.

Points to make clear

About current

❏ Empty cups must be returned to keep the flow going. This is like using a chain of buckets to get water from a river to put out a fire.

About energy

❏ If the wheel is to be made to spin faster, more water/energy must be supplied and the water in the bucket is used more quickly.

❏ To supply more water, the cups must be transferred more quickly; two cups could be passed by each person, or the cups could be full instead of half full. These equate to increased current in the circuit.

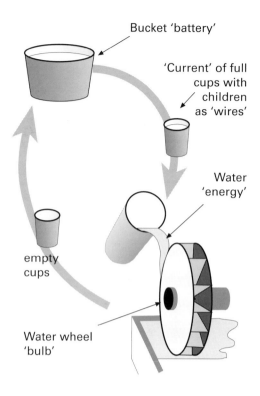

Bucket 'battery'

'Current' of full cups with children as 'wires'

Water 'energy'

empty cups

Water wheel 'bulb'

Disadvantages and limitations

❏ Synchronised passing of the cups is essential here.

❏ The 'current' goes *to* the sink rather than *through* it.

❏ May lead to a view of energy as a substance.

Variations

Other 'carrier' models include the giant's castle, which can form the basis of a story supported by a diagram. The castle and the mine are linked by a circular railway. In the mine, miners continuously load coal into trucks and push them along the rails to the castle. The coal is used to heat and light the castle and the trucks return to the mine. The mine and miners represent the battery, the moving trucks the current, and the fuel the energy. If the trucks are linked, moving one truck will cause all to move simultaneously around the track. This model can lead to 'thought experiments' about how to get more energy to the castle.

A4   The circle of string

Representation of the physical circuit

Battery represented by person moving the string.

Wires represented by hands providing the pathway.

Bulb represented by person gripping the string.

Representation of current and energy

Current represented by moving string.

Energy has no physical representation.

'Bulb' lightly grips the string

'Wires' are the hands that provide a pathway for the string

BULB

'Battery' moves the string

Moving string is the 'current'

Points to make clear

About current

❏ The string is present all the time, in the whole circuit, but only moves when the 'battery person' makes it move. In the same way the electrons, which move when a current flows, are already in the metal wires but nothing happens until a battery is connected.

❏ The string in all parts of the circuit starts moving simultaneously, and at the same speed everywhere. Current either flows in the circuit or it does not; it cannot be flowing in part of the circuit only.

❏ The same amount of string leaves the battery as returns to it. It does not get used up on the way. In the same way current does not get used up.

About energy

❏ If the 'battery person' keeps moving the string, he/she will use energy and get tired.

❏ The 'bulb person' (person who grips the string) feels his/her hand get hot, so energy has been transferred from the battery person to the string to make it move, and from the moving string to the hands of the bulb person gripping it. No-one else feels any real heating effect because they are not resisting the movement of the string

❏ In a circuit the only significant energy transfer is where there is a resistance to the flow of current. The thin filament in the bulb has a high resistance and so causes a transfer of energy.

❏ A battery of higher voltage can be represented by a person giving the string a bigger push, transferring more energy to it and making it move faster, and so increasing the rate at which energy is supplied to the bulb.

❏ The dual role of the battery in providing energy to the components of the circuit and providing the 'push' which makes the current flow, is thus demonstrated.

About resistance

❏ If everyone in the circle grips the string tightly, there is a very high resistance and the string will not move. This represents the situation in an electrical insulator.

❏ The resistance in a circuit affects the flow of current in the whole circuit.

Disadvantages and limitations

❏ A switch as a break in the circuit cannot easily be demonstrated, since if the string is cut it can continue to be moved for some time.

Points to make clear

❑ Analogies help us to think, but they all have strengths and weaknesses. Nothing behaves exactly like electricity in a circuit.

❑ Identify the physical relationships between the analogy and a real circuit first. What represents the bulb, the battery, the wires?

❑ We can think of the battery as a source of energy. This energy is carried to the bulb, where it is transferred to the surroundings as heat and light. These ideas about energy fit comfortably with the 'source-consumer' model and with children's intuitive ideas about energy as something that 'makes things happen'.

❑ The current, flowing continuously around the circuit, provides the means by which energy is transferred from the battery to the bulb.

❑ Batteries are much safer than mains electricity because they only deliver a relatively small current.

Use of ideas, applications and extensions

1 Use the analogies, once introduced, to support thinking when trying to explain observations which are problematic, such as:

  ❑ why two bulbs in series are dimmer than one

  ❑ why two bulbs in series are equally as dim as each other.

The available energy from the battery must be equally shared between the bulbs. However, this leads to the question of how the current 'knows' to share the energy and doesn't just give up all its energy to the first bulb. Of course, the current does not 'know'. The situation can be imagined by thinking about what would happen in the Smartie analogy. If there were two obstacles and all the energy had been transferred at the first one, the 'current' would be unable to pass the second obstacle and the circuit would not operate.

2 Test the ideas. From the model, we can predict that the current is the same at all points in the circuit and test this using ammeters. The readings obtained support the explanatory model introduced.

Simply introducing an analogy will not help children to understand a circuit better. However, highlighting the challenges to a simple source-consumer model, together with well-chosen practical work and the use of ideas of current and energy, will help children to move forward in their thinking.

7 Light

7.1 The behaviour of light

National Curriculum reference
Sc 4 Physical processes
Pupils should be taught:
KS1   3a to identify different light sources, including the Sun
       3b that darkness is the absence of light
KS2   3a that light travels from a source
       3b that light cannot pass through some materials, and how this leads to the formation of shadows
       3c that light is reflected from surfaces (for example, mirrors, polished metals)
       3d that we see things only when light from them enters our eyes

Scottish National Guidelines
Environmental studies. Properties and uses of energy
Level C   link light to shadow formation
          give examples of light being reflected from surfaces

Relevant QCA units
1D   Light and dark
3F   Light and shadows
6F   How we see things

What's the problem?

Moving from describing observable effects to explaining them involves developing a conceptual model which includes the ideas that:

■ light travels

■ light travels in straight lines

■ travelling light can be represented by lines called rays.

What might children think?

Children are likely to:

❏ be able to identify many different sources of light, but think there are different kinds of light, such as electric light, daylight, sunlight, and may think these behave differently

❏ know and use the word 'light' in a number of contexts and with several meanings. It can be a noun (the light), a verb (to light) or an adjective (light blue). It may be associated with a source of light, patch of light, brightness of a place or object, shade of colour or weight (as in heavy and light).

❏ think of light as a state (this room is light), but may not think that it moves

❏ know that they can see lit rooms or car headlights more clearly at night and may think that light travels further at night, rather than that this is due to contrast effects

❏ use the word 'shine' when talking about light, e.g. 'The Sun shines on us' or 'I can see the torch shining on the wall' but may be simply referring to an observed effect and not necessarily to light travelling.

The challenge for the teacher

The teacher needs to:

❏ help children to move from simply describing what happens to being able to offer explanations and make predictions based on these

❏ support the development of a conceptual model to enable this to happen.

Vocabulary

In addition to the everyday uses of the word 'light' mentioned above, other words used in this chapter which have both scientific and everyday meanings include:

❏ 'ray' which children may associate with comic strips and 'death rays'

❏ reflection, which in everyday use is what is seen, that is, an image. Scientifically it is a process in which the direction of a beam of light is changed, and the process by which we see objects and colour.

Possible starting points

Use familiar phenomena to encourage children to think about the implications of what we take for granted. To focus children's attention on the idea that the light must *move* from the thing which produces it to where it can be seen, ask questions such as:

❏ how does light from the Sun form a patch on the floor?

❏ how can the torch make a bright spot on the wall?

❏ how does the overhead projector make a bright patch on the screen?

Focus | Light travels

Ideas of light travelling, and travelling in straight lines, could be introduced by:

1 Discussion of pictures or experiences of beams of sunlight passing through a dusty room, trees in a wood or gaps in clouds.

2 Using children's knowledge of situations in which light is used to send information, e.g. lighthouses or Morse code.

3 Using children's knowledge of car headlights or laser shows when beams can be seen.

4 Using chalk dust to make the path of light from a source such as an overhead projector visible (care!).

5 'Catching' light as it travels, by putting a piece of card between the source and the screen.

6 Asking children to predict what they will see, by drawing on paper under the box, when a light source, centrally placed under a circular box with slits in the sides, is switched on (Figure 7.1). This is very effective in a darkened room.

7 'Bouncing' light around the classroom using mirrors and following its path.

8 Arranging boards with holes in, so that light shone in at one end can emerge and hit a screen. This can only happen if all holes are in line. Discuss what happens to the light if one hole is not in line with the others (Figure 7.2).

9 Utilising any opportunities for 'total darkness' experiences, e.g. during trips to mines or caves. Drawing children's attention to any shafts of light, and the effects of small light sources in the darkness.

10 In a darkened room, looking for evidence of light from a small source, such as a candle or small light bulb, reaching surfaces. How does it get there?

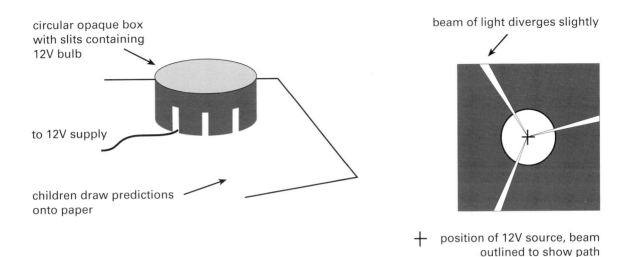

circular opaque box
with slits containing
12V bulb

to 12V supply

children draw predictions
onto paper

beam of light diverges slightly

+ position of 12V source, beam
outlined to show path

7.1 *Where will the light be seen? General view of equipment and effect as seen from above.*

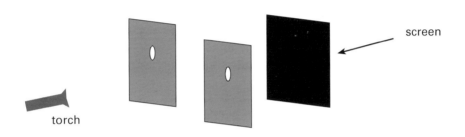

screen

torch

7.2 *When the light is switched on, how must the holes be aligned so that light can reach the screen?*

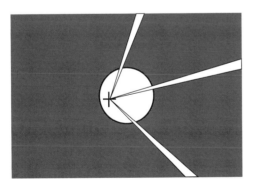

7.3 *The path of light when the source is not in the centre of the box*

Points to make clear

❏ Light does not 'go' in the way that a road or a washing line 'goes' from one place to another. However, some children may interpret their observations and discussions of light travelling in this way. To help them to think of light 'going' like a thrown ball, it may be helpful for them to be encouraged to think about what happens when a bulb is switched on and off very quickly (as in the Morse code example 2 above). What happens to the 'bit' of light that is produced?

❏ When using mirrors, keep the focus on what happens to the light, rather than what can be seen in the mirror.

❏ Drawings or models which represent the path of light can help to clarify thinking (*see* Focus: Representing light below).

❏ In example 6 above, many children will intuitively predict a straight-line path, at right angles to the surface, although the light is often visible over a much greater distance than they expect! How did they know it would be like this? What does this suggest about how light travels? What would we see if light didn't travel in straight lines? Discussing and drawing the path of the light if the source is not centrally placed (Figure 7.3) allows both reinforcement of ideas about the straight line path and the use of lines to represent the path of light. These lines can then be termed 'rays' and, with arrows, indicate direction of travel.

Focus | Representing light

Travelling light can be represented using various physical means.

1 Modelling the direction of movement of the light with hands when talking about light travelling from a source.

2 Using static models in which spaghetti, string, or coloured paper glued on to a black background can show the path of light (Figure 7.4).

3 Using white or yellow spray paint on black card. Putting an object between the can (which represents the light source) and the card (which represents the screen) means some paint is blocked and no paint (light) reaches the card. The resulting black shape is the shadow.

4 Using dynamic models, such as balls (representing light) rolling in a straight line towards a wall when there is an obstacle in the way. Where can the light reach to?

5 Children walking in straight lines and being stopped by, or passing, an object allows them to 'be' the light.

Such strategies can lead into the conventional representation of light using straight lines, with arrows to indicate direction.

Points to make clear

❏ Most representations (string, lines, etc.) have the disadvantage that they are of finite length and stop in a way that a light ray does not.

❏ When moving children find their path blocked by an object, they stop. This can lead to an interesting discussion about what happens to light. (It is absorbed or reflected.)

❏ If paint is sprayed on an object the paint collects on the surface. Light does not do this (see above).

Conventional representation

The conventional representation of light, as seen in textbooks when explaining phenomena such as reflection, refraction or vision, consists of lines representing selected rays with arrows representing direction. Building up a conceptual model in ways which encourage children to think of light travelling in straight lines, rather than just presenting diagrams as explanations themselves, is likely to make them more confident in their understanding, both of phenomena and of such representations.

Use of ideas, applications and extensions

When something is in the way of light it may be blocked, leading to the formation of a shadow, it may be sent in a different direction (reflection), or it may pass through. Children have a great deal of experience of shadows, but have rarely observed their behaviour in any systematic way or thought about how to explain it.

Both shadow formation and reflection provide opportunities to use the conceptual model to explain observed effects.

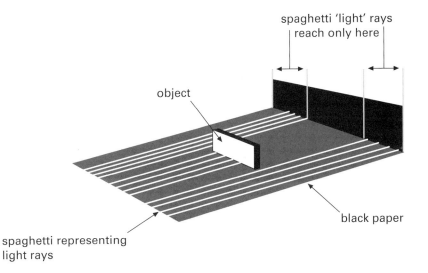

spaghetti 'light' rays
reach only here

object

black paper

spaghetti representing
light rays

7.4 *Spaghetti model to show light paths*

Shadow

Across my bedroom wall

flapping its giant grey wings:

a monster

Across my bedroom lamp

fluttering its small brown wings:

a moth

7.5 *Shadow*

'Shadow' by Michael Rosen from *STAR* Science, Technology and Reading – a resource for teachers (2000)* ASE

Focus | **Shadows**

As the formation of shadows is a piece of evidence which supports the idea of light travelling in straight lines, it is worth considering whether the conceptual model should be introduced *before* work on shadows. This allows children to focus on the use of the model to explain their observations and to make predictions, rather than on the phenomenon of shadows *per se*.

Challenge children to use the model to:

1 Explain observations such as:

- ❏ how their shadow is produced on a sunny day
- ❏ the change in shadow length and position during the day
- ❏ the change in shadow length when walking away from a street light
- ❏ how small objects can produce large shadows. The poem, 'Shadow', can be a useful stimulus to discussion (Figure **7.5**)
- ❏ how an object can have more than one shadow. Children may have noticed this, for example, when watching floodlit football matches
- ❏ how eclipses happen.

2 Make and test predictions:
- ❏ what will happen to the size of the shadow as the object moves away from the source?
- ❏ how big will the shadow be when the source is at different heights?

3 Produce interesting effects:
- ❏ an object with two or three shadows
- ❏ a coloured shadow
- ❏ a large and a small object with shadows the same size.

Points to make clear

❏ Children's attention may need to be drawn to the fact that the source is always on the opposite side of the object to the shadow.

❏ Some children confuse shadows and reflections. They may draw shadows with features and detail, or consider that they are somehow projected out of the object. Understanding that shadows are formed when light is blocked by an object, but that reflections are formed when light is 'bounced' off in a different direction, is an important distinction.

❏ In the poem, note that the shadow can be much bigger than the moth and this depends on the distance between the moth and the lamp. The moth is brown but the shadow is grey. In reality, because the light source is bigger than the moth, the shadow is unlikely to be very clear.

❏ A lunar eclipse is when the Moon passes through the Earth's shadow. A solar eclipse is when the Earth passes through the Moon's shadow.

Focus | ## The reflection of light

When light hits an object and cannot pass through it, children may know that a shadow is formed, but what happens to the light?

1 Use good examples of light being reflected to emphasise that when light hits an object, it may be 'bounced' off. Represent the path of the light in a diagram, e.g. the 'dazzle' of sunlight from a shiny watch on a sunny day.

2 Play team games, e.g. 'Hit the target'. One person has a torch, the others (start with one and build up to three or four people) have mirrors. Light must be 'passed' from one to the other to hit a target.

3 Use ball games to model the behaviour of light, e.g. throwing a ball against a wall for a partner to catch, bouncing balls on the floor to a partner. Link this to the path of a beam of light travelling from a torch to a reflector to a 'detector', e.g. a piece of card, or the target in the game.

4 Shine a torch into one end of a periscope, with the other end pointed at a screen. Draw the path of the light (Figure **7.6**).

Points to make clear

❏ When light hits something and can't go through, it can be bounced off. This is reflection. The direction of the light is changed.

❏ We use periscopes to allow us to 'see over things'. Talking in this way can reinforce the notion of an 'active eye'. Shining the torch in at one end and seeing light come out at the other focuses attention on the path of the light.

❏ Distinguish between reflection, in the sense of changing the direction in which light travels, and *a* reflection, the image seen in a mirror. Keep the focus on the behaviour of the light, as the formation of images is complex.

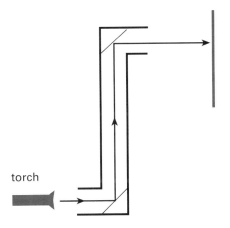

7.6 *The periscope*

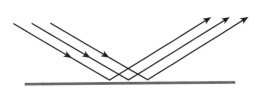

regular reflection at smooth surface

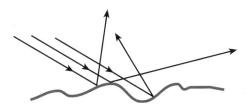

scattering at rough surface

7.7 *Reflection and scattering*

Use of ideas, applications and extensions
Children could be asked to use their knowledge to:

1 explain how the 'cats-eyes' in the road work

2 explain why a real cat's eyes seem to shine in the dark

3 explore how we use reflecting surfaces to help us

4 design and make a periscope, or a device to see round corners.

Focus | **All objects reflect light**

This is a difficult concept, but it is necessary in order to understand how we see. It is advisable not to introduce it unless children are fairly confident about reflection at shiny surfaces and that we see light sources when light from them enters our eyes.

1 Use tinfoil as a reflector. When it is smooth, what happens to light shone on to it? What happens when it is crumpled up?

2 Use pictures of clear reflections in water. Why does the surface of the water need to be undisturbed?

3 Do you like butter? How is it that buttercups make our skin glow yellow? Use brightly coloured card to produce different colours.

4 Model the behaviour of light meeting a rough surface by bouncing balls on rough ground.

7.8 *Concept cartoon – the white cat problem*

reduced, from Keogh and Naylor, *Concept Cartoons in Science Education*, 2000

Points to make clear

❑ Smooth surfaces reflect light from a source regularly to the eye, so that an image is seen.

❑ Rough surfaces also reflect light but *scatter* it in all directions (see Figure **7.7**).

❑ Buttercups reflect yellow light, which can be seen on the skin.

❑ If objects did not reflect light, we would be unable to see them. Some children may make the links to black holes in space. Since these are areas of space from which no light can escape, they can only be seen due to contrast with areas around them.

Use of ideas, applications and extensions

Children can be asked to use their knowledge to:

❑ explain how we see the moon

❑ think about the concept cartoon 'The white cat' (see Figure **7.8**)

❑ draw diagrams which explain how we see objects such as books, or trees.

7.2 How we see

National Curriculum reference
Sc4 Physical processes
KS2   3d that we see things only when light from them enters our eyes

Scottish National Guidelines
Environmental studies. Properties and uses of energy
Level B   link light … to seeing …

Relevant QCA units
6F   How we see things

What's the problem?

■ Recognising that our eyes, like other sense organs, receive information from our surroundings.

■ Using ideas about light travelling to understand the relationship between a source, an object and the eye.

What might children think?

Children know we use our eyes to see but may:

❑ think light simply helps us to see better

❑ have 'active eye' ideas about vision and think something travels from the eye to the object

❑ think that light from light sources enters the eye, but that we see other objects because our eyes send out something to them.

The challenge for the teacher

The teacher needs to:

❑ introduce the eye as a receptor (detector) of light

❑ help children to see similarities between different sense organs. They all receive information from our surroundings and pass messages to the brain for interpretation, but what is received varies (light, chemicals, etc.).

❑ draw on ideas of light travelling to explain how we see.

Vocabulary

Many everyday expressions reinforce the idea of an 'active eye', such as 'piercing blue eyes', 'giving dirty looks' and being unable to 'see through' someone. Talking about transparent materials as 'see through', rather than letting light through, can reinforce this idea.

Introduce essential terms, e.g. pupil, iris, etc.

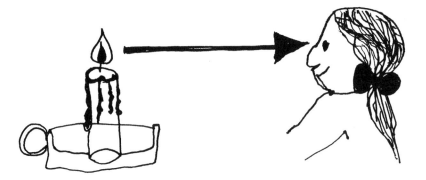

7.9 *Child's drawing of how we see a candle*

Possible starting points

1 Raise questions such as:

- ❏ why is it dangerous to look at the Sun even through black glass?
- ❏ how do sunglasses help us to see in bright light (but do NOT allow us to look safely at the Sun)?
- ❏ when have you been dazzled? How did you respond?
- ❏ why do drivers dip their headlights?
- ❏ why do people use blindfolds to help them sleep on planes?

⚠ HAZARD

Focus on the fact that too much light entering our eyes can make it difficult to see or may damage our eyes, and that we can use things to control how much light gets to our eyes.

2 Discuss our senses. What can our bodies detect? Which parts of us detect what? Children know that they taste something when it is put in their mouths. What has to enter our ears, our noses, our eyes?

Focus

We see when light enters our eyes

1 Have children observe the changes to the pupil in the eye of a partner under normal light, when the eye is covered for a few seconds and then uncovered, and when a bright light is shone near to (but not at) the eye.

Relate this to children's experience of going into a darkened room, when it takes some time for eyes to adjust.

2 Ask children to draw how they think they see a candle, or other bright light. Discuss the drawings and ensure children can use an arrow to represent the path of light travelling from the source to the eye (Figure **7.9**).

3 Challenge children to draw how light from different sources gets to the eye in a range of situations, e.g.

- ❏ looking in a mirror at a torch held behind them
- ❏ using a periscope to look at a candle over a barrier
- ❏ using a mirror to see a lamp round a corner
- ❏ looking at a streetlight through a window.

Ask them to think about how to explain the effect of blindfolds, sunglasses, etc.

Points to make clear

❏ Emphasise that the pupil is a hole which allows light to enter the eye. The size of the hole is changed, by the iris, to control the amount of light entering the eye. When we enter a darkened room the pupil gets bigger to allow more light to enter. In total darkness, however big the pupil gets, we will be unable to see because there is no light to enter the eye.

❏ A good blindfold will stop all the light before it reaches the eye, so we will be unable to see anything. Sunglasses reduce the amount of light entering our eyes, a window allows almost all light to pass through.

Use of ideas, applications and extensions

Once children are confident about explaining how we see light sources in a range of situations, they can move on to thinking about how we see other objects (see Section **7.1** *The behaviour of light*, Focus: All objects reflect light, page 61).

HAZARD

Discuss health and safety issues about light radiation, and include sunglasses bearing the CE code limiting the amount of harmful ultraviolet radiation entering the eye. Of course sunglasses do NOT protect the skin – hence sunburn and possibly skin cancer, unless the skin is protected.

REFERENCES AND FURTHER READING

Chapter   1 Introduction

[1] Many books on primary science contain chapters which discuss the nature of science and the purposes of science education. Examples include:

Harlen, W. (2000) *Teaching, learning and assessing science 5 –12*. 3rd edn. London: Paul Chapman.

Newton, L. D. (2000) *Meeting the standards in primary science*. Chapter 2 'What do we mean by the nature of science?' London: Routledge Falmer.

Ratcliffe, M. (1998) 'The purposes of science education' in Sherington, R. (ed.) *ASE guide to primary science education*. Cheltenham: Stanley Thornes.

[2] Useful summaries of children's ideas about a wide range of topics can be found in:

Driver, R., Squires, A., Rushworth, P. and Wood-Robinson, V. (1994) *Making sense of secondary science: research into children's ideas*. London: Routledge.

Primary SPACE Project Research Reports. *Growth* (1990), *Light* (1990), *Sound* (1990), *Evaporation and condensation* (1990), *Materials* (1991), *Electricity* (1991), *Processes of life* (1992), *Rocks, soil and weather* (1992), *Forces* (1998). Liverpool University Press.

(SPACE stands for Science Processes and Concept Exploration)

[3] Books on primary science often contain chapters which explore children's learning, and the implications for teaching. Examples include:

Harlen, W. (2000) *Teaching, learning and assessing science 5 –12*. 3rd edn. London: Paul Chapman.

Ollerenshaw, C. and Ritchie, R. (1997) *Primary science: making it work*. 2nd edn. London: Fulton.

Vosniadou, S. (1997) 'On the development of the understanding of abstract ideas'. Chapter 2 in Harnqvist, K. and Burgen, A. (eds) *Growing up with science: developing early understanding of science*. London: Kingsley.

Watt, D. (1998) 'Children's learning of science concepts' in Sherington, R. (ed.) *ASE guide to primary science education*. Cheltenham: Stanley Thornes.

A broad range of issues, including 'constructivist' views, are discussed in:

Hodson, D. (1998) *Teaching and learning science*. Buckingham: Open University Press.

The limitations of practical experience and arguments for explicitly presenting the science view to children are explored in:

Driver, R., Asoko, H., Leach, J., Mortimer, E. and Scott, P. (1994) 'Constructing scientific knowledge in the classroom', *Educational Researcher*, **23**(7), 5–12.

[4] Explaining, and teaching for understanding, are discussed by:

Newton, L. D. (2000) *Meeting the standards in primary science*. In Chapter 9, 'What do we mean by teaching for understanding?' London: Routledge Falmer.

Ogborn, J., Kress, G., Martins, I. and McGillicuddy, K. (1996) *Explaining science in the classroom*. Buckingham: Open University Press.

Wragg, E. C. and Brown, G. (1993) *Explaining*. London: Routledge.

[5] ASE (1993) *Models and modelling in science education*. Hatfield: Association for Science Education (out of print).

[6] de Bóo, M. and Asoko, H. (2000) Using models, analogies and illustrations to help children think about science ideas. *Primary Science Review*, **65**, 25–28.

[7] Goswami, U. (1998) *Cognition in children*. Hove: Psychology Press.

[8] Sutton, C. (1992) *Words, science and learning*. Buckingham: Open University Press.

Chapter   2 Green plants

[1] Simon Bailey, Head of Science Education at Crewe and Alsager Faculty of Manchester Metropolitan University, designed the Eco-game. Bailey, S. (1995) Developing ecological understanding through drama: the Eco game. *Primary Science Review*, **38**, 11–13.

2.1 Further reading

Russell, T. and Watt, D. (1990) Primary SPACE Project Research Reports: *Growth*. Liverpool University Press.

Nuffield Primary Science/SPACE (1993) *The variety of life*. London: Collins Educational.

2.3 Further reading

Barker and Carr (1989) (in Driver *et al.*, see [2] above, 30–31) on photosynthesis: *'The view that plants' food is the material they absorb is resistant to change even in the face of continued instruction'*.

Chapter 3 The human body

Osborne, J., Wadsworth, P. and Black, P. (1992) Primary SPACE Project Research Reports: *Processes of life*. Liverpool University Press.

Sizmur, S. and Ashby, J. (1997) *Introducing scientific concepts to children*. NFER.

Chapter 4 Materials

[1] Oversby, J. (2000) Good explanations for dissolving – even expert chemists find this hard! *Primary Science Review*, **63**, 16–19.

[2] Driver, R., Squires, A., Rushworth, P. and Wood-Robinson, V. (1994) *Making sense of secondary science: research into children's ideas*. London: Routledge .

[3] Russell, T., Longden, K. and McGuigan, L. (1991) Primary SPACE Project Research Reports: *Materials*. Liverpool University Press.

[4] Wright, L. and Wiggins, D. (1996–2000) *ASE 5-year Study*. Hatfield: The Association for Science Education.

Further reading

Warwick, P. and Stephenson, P. (2000) Heat and changing materials. *Primary Science Review*, **63**, 4–7.

Chapter 5 Forces

Kruger, C., Palacio, D. and Summers, M. (1991) *Understanding forces*. Oxford University Department of Educational Studies and Westminster College, Oxford.

Russell, T., McGuigan, L. and Hughes, A. (1998) Primary SPACE Project Research Reports: *Forces*. Liverpool University Press.

Simon, S., Black, P., Blondel, E. and Brown, M. (1994) *Forces in balance*. Hatfield: Association for Science Education.

Chapter 6 Electricity

Asoko, H. (1996) Developing scientific concepts in the primary classroom: teaching about electric circuits. In Welford, G., Osborne, J. and Scott, P. (eds) *Research in science education in Europe*. pp. 36–49. The Falmer Press.

Jabin, Z. and Smith, R. (1994) Using analogies of electricity flow in circuits to improve understanding. *Primary Science Review*, **35**, 23–26.

Newton, L. and Newton, D. (1996) Young children and understanding electricity. *Primary Science Review*, **41**, 14–16.

Osborne, J., Black, P., Smith, M. and Meadows, J. (1991) Primary SPACE Project Research Reports: *Electricity*. Liverpool University Press.

Parker, J. and Heywood, D. (1996) Circuit training – towards the notion of a complete circuit. *Primary Science Review*, **41**, 16–18.

Qualter, A. (1994) Where does electricity come from? *Primary Science Review*, **35**, 20–22.

Summers, M., Kruger, C. and Mant, J. (1997) *Teaching electricity effectively: a research based guide for primary science*. Hatfield: Association for Science Education.

Chapter 7 Light

Naylor, R. and Peacock, A. (2000) I saw bubbles in my head. *Primary Science Review*, **61**, 11–14

Osborne, J., Black, P., Smith, M. and Meadows, J. (1990) Primary SPACE Project Research Reports: *Light*. Liverpool University Press.